LIFE
THROUGH THE
ARCHES

KEN BROWN

LIFE
THROUGH THE
ARCHES

SIX FREEDOM PRINCIPLES FOR SUCCESSFUL ENTREPRENEURS

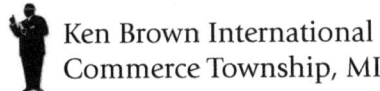

Ken Brown International
Commerce Township, MI

LIFE through the Arches
by Ken Brown

Published by Ken Brown International
3050 Union Lake Road
Suite 8-F
Commerce Township, MI 48382
(248) 240-0646
www.kenbrowninternational.com

This book or parts thereof may not be reproduced in any form, stored in a retrieval system, or transmitted in any form by any means—electronic, mechanical, photocopy, recording, or otherwise—without prior written permission of the publisher, except as provided by United States of America copyright law.

Unless otherwise identified, scripture quotations are from The New King James Version (NKJV®), copyright 1979, 1980, 1982, Thomas Nelson, Inc., Publishers.

Scripture quotations marked NIV are taken from The Holy Bible, New International Version (NIV). Copyright ©1973, 1978, 1984, International Bible Society. Used by permission of Zondervan Bible Publishers.

Copyright © 2011 by Ken Brown
All rights reserved.

ISBN 13: 9780976874294
Cover Design: LaTanya Orr

First Edition
10 11 12 13 — 9 8 7 6 5 4 3 2 1

Printed in the United States of America

Table of Contents

One: True Freedom 1

Faith
Two: Ground Zero of Business Success 13
Three: The Journey of Creativity 23
Four: Working It 35

Vision
Five: The Glorious Image in Their Heads 51
Six: Staying Out of the Ditch 63
Seven: Everything in Its Season 73

Purpose
Eight: Answering the Why 87
Nine: People before Profits 99
Ten: The Custom of Success 115

Passion
Eleven: Monday Morning Heart Attack 131
Twelve: Finding the Diamonds 143
Thirteen: Superman 155

Ownership
Fourteen: Destroy the Ships 169
Fifteen: Doing What It Takes 181
Sixteen: A Balanced Life 195

Associations
Seventeen: Iron Sharpens Iron 211
Eighteen: Soaking up Knowledge 225
Nineteen: The Right Dream Needs the Right People 235

Final Freedom Thoughts
Green and Growing 249

ONE
True Freedom

I was fourteen years old when we were evicted from my uncle's ice cream store. My mother, sisters, and I had been living there, in the back room. But my uncle hadn't kept up with the rent, so we had to leave. By then we had become experienced with moving on. We had already been evicted from several homes and had lived with several other relatives. We lived on welfare and struggled to maintain a normal life.

From my uncle's store, we walked down Seventy-ninth Street, carrying our bags of clothing. Seventy-ninth Street was not a place you wanted to be. It was known for seediness and crime. We trudged past liquor stores, pawnshops, and check-cashing centers. We walked along the broken concrete sidewalk where, later, gangs and drug dealers would claim their nighttime territory.

The next stop in our nomadic life was the apartment of my uncle's girlfriend, Miss Pearl. She lived at the corner of Seventy-ninth and Ashland Avenue and was kind enough to take us in temporarily. She escorted us to her apartment and unlocked the metal security gate that protected her front door. Then she unlocked the door and let us in. Light shone into the apartment through the bars on her window. We piled our bags in a corner on her living room floor—the same floor we later used for a bed. We had no home and no money, and I felt locked behind the bars of the window and the gate. I did not feel free. It felt like the end of the road.

But it wasn't the end. It was just the beginning—the beginning of great things to come.

Fast-forward twenty years. By then I had graduated from college. I had enjoyed a successful career in the food industry and dreamed of opening my own restaurant. By following certain life principles, and through the love of supportive people, I overcame the poverty and obstacles of my youth. I was living in freedom!

In my last book, *LIFE: Living in Freedom Everyday*, I introduced six life principles I formulated through my earlier experiences, which propelled me along the road of freedom. To achieve success, I had to have *faith, vision, purpose*, and *passion*. In addition, I had to take *ownership* of my life and *associate* with people who would lift me up and not keep me down. That was the only way I could escape from poverty.

Those principles worked for me—beyond my wildest dreams. By the time I was only thirty-four years old, I took ownership of two McDonald's restaurants. My entrepreneurial vision had come true. Although I had achieved success up to that point, there was no guarantee it would continue once I became an owner. It was my dream, but I would face many obstacles. In some ways, it was like living at Miss Pearl's again. At first, I didn't have much to call my own—no staff, no employees, and no business plan. I had just moved to Michigan from Chicago, and my family had yet to join me. I knew few people in the state. I was alone. I felt as vulnerable as I did sleeping on the floor of that apartment.

To succeed, I relied again on those six principles that had enabled me to overcome the challenges of my childhood.

Fast-forward nine more years. One December evening, I attended a party with a hundred other people—a room full of colleagues, employees (past and present), customers, family members, and friends. They were there to celebrate my retirement at the age of forty-three. They cheered and gave speeches and celebrated the success we had achieved together.

I had sold my two restaurants to the tune of $4.4 million. In fact, I sold one of the stores for more money than any McDonald's in Michigan had ever sold for. I had dramatically increased the annual sales of both restaurants to more than $5 million. I had taken one old, underperforming restaurant, and one new restaurant with an inexperienced staff, and turned them into two of the highest performing restaurants in the region.

But my success wasn't just about money. Through entrepreneurship, I was given the opportunity to make a difference in people's lives.

At the retirement party, Kevin Butts, an entrepreneur in my network of fellow business owners, said, "Across the city of Detroit, Ken has had one of the most profound impacts on this community, especially among young African American men and women."

One of my managers, Robert Smith, added, "I've worked with many operators during my twenty-three years with McDonald's. But I've never worked with an owner who has such a pulse on the people. He is a man who always puts his people before his profits."

My vision had been to develop my business into a role model for outstanding restaurant operations. And I succeeded! But how did I achieve this success with my entrepreneurial dream? I didn't achieve it by getting a finance degree first. I didn't achieve it by ruthlessly driving my employees to succeed. And I didn't achieve it through a detailed knowledge of marketing. I did it by strictly adhering to the same six freedom principles of success.

Today, I've moved on to my next entrepreneurial vision. I am a life and business coach, speaking to large groups and working with people one-on-one to teach them how those principles can give us freedom—the freedom to live a full life every day, and the freedom to achieve our entrepreneurial dreams.

Are you ready to experience the freedom of entrepreneurship? Would you like to open a business or buy an existing one? Would you like to turn your passion into profits, but you are nervous about starting? Or are you already an entrepreneur, but you'd like to take your venture to the next level? Do you still have that burning desire to be a successful entrepreneur but don't yet have the know-how or the mind-set to pull it off? Then keep reading. This book will provide a road map to get you to your next level.

Many people go into business ownership because they desire greater freedom. They want to be their own boss, but then the responsibilities of ownership overwhelm them. Or they want financial independence, but then that desire morphs into obsessive micromanagement and putting profits first. For many entrepreneurs, true freedom is elusive.

Many budding entrepreneurs miss the need for having a freedom plan to achieve success. Financial wealth alone does not provide freedom—just look at the many wealthy people who live unhappy lives. In order for entrepreneurs to find happiness, they must live their lives and run their businesses a certain way.

Within these pages, I will not cover the intricate details of writing a business plan. I will not walk you through how to get an SBA loan. I will not compare and contrast the most effective marketing techniques. Those are important things to know, and there are many great books that discuss the finer mechanics of running a business. This book is different.

Life through the Arches discusses factors rarely taught in business schools, yet absolutely essential to achieving success *and* happiness. These aspects of success are ignored too often by entrepreneurs who fail, or just as bad, ignored by entrepreneurs who grow rich but at too high a cost to themselves, their employees, and their families. Within these pages, you'll read about my life through the Golden Arches of McDonald's and how I specifically applied these six principles to achieve incredible success. You'll also read how those principles can be applied to any business venture. Through faith, vision, purpose, passion, ownership, and associations, you will succeed.

Faith

The first requirement for successful business ownership is faith. Entrepreneurs must have faith in themselves, in their employees, and most important, faith in the Lord. God designed each of us to be creative beings, and he has given us everything we need to be successful. Unfortunately, fear often constrains many entrepreneurs.

As a business owner, you will enjoy wonderful mountaintop experiences, yet also you will face obstacles and challenging valley experiences. Fear will trap you in those valleys. But an unyielding belief in God and yourself will help you walk through them so you can arrive at the next mountain.

Faith directs us to creative solutions. It keeps us targeted on our goals. It gives us joy and allows us to live a life without regrets.

Vision

What does your future business look like to you? Or have you crystallized a vision of the future of your current business? Do you know where you are headed?

Knowing where you are going—having a picture in your mind—allows you to dream big and act boldly. As entrepreneurs, we must visualize our business just like a track-andfield athlete visualizes winning the race. A large profit is not a vision—an athlete doesn't visualize standing with the trophy, but he visualizes the race. Likewise, successful entrepreneurs develop a detailed vision of what their dream looks like, and profit becomes the fruit of following that vision.

Without a vision, the Bible says, people will perish.[1] So will a business. As a business coach, I have witnessed too many aimless businesses driven to the brink of failure due to a lack of visual imagination.

Purpose

Just as with vision, making a profit is not the purpose of an entrepreneur. Our purpose isn't even to build a successful business. Our purpose is to follow God's calling on our lives and to make a difference. Impact drives income! We are called to live a life of significance and provide a valuable experience or product to our customers.

We need to make a difference in the lives of our external customers—the ones buying our products or services. The typical company loses half of its customers

---
1. See Proverbs 29:18.

every five years. Customer service, in general, is in terrible shape right now. People want to be treated right. And they want their lives improved (even in small ways) by spending money on what you offer.

We also need to make a difference in the lives of our internal customers—our employees—the people delivering what we sell. Our employees are our greatest asset, and we need to develop them and improve their lives.

Passion

When we are in sync with our God-given gifts, we get a fire in the belly that drives us to succeed. The desire to be our own boss, or the longing to get out of a bad job situation, doesn't provide us with lasting passion. Nor is passion found by following the latest business trend in the *Wall Street Journal*. Passion is found inside of us.

When people stick with jobs or follow business ventures that don't align with their gifts, they fall victim to indifference and procrastination—two of the most potent business killers. Passion and a lack of passion are both contagious. Customers and employees sense when there's no energy and optimism in a business, and they will eventually turn away from it. But passionate entrepreneurs draw enthusiastic customers and valuable employees to their businesses. Passionate entrepreneurs will set themselves on fire, and people will pay to watch them burn.

True Freedom

Ownership

Of course entrepreneurs *own* their business. But that's not the most important type of ownership. Entrepreneurs are the CEOs of their lives. We must be intentional about our thoughts, habits, and actions. We need to remember to cast a leader's shadow. Our employees will determine what is most important not by what we say but by what we do—especially when we don't think anyone is watching.

We also must take 100 percent responsibility for learning new things and becoming subject-matter experts. We must establish our personal brand. Brands like McDonald's and Coca-Cola are known the world over for specific things. How will you be different? What expertise will set you apart?

We also need to take 100 percent responsibility for how we spend our time. To be successful, entrepreneurs must live balanced lives. We cannot be wed to the business 24/7 but must also spend quality time focusing on our families, communities, and spirituality.

Associations

Who influences you the most? Do you pay attention to the type of people you hang with? Entrepreneurs carry a lot of responsibility on their backs, and they can feel isolated from peers. People who discourage and deplete us, even if they are family members or good friends, can hurt our chances of success. Although it can be hard to do, we must minimize our associations with people who bring us down. However, by developing healthy associations with people who encourage and teach us, we can climb to the next level.

You don't need to hang with a bunch of yes men. You need to hang with people who will support and challenge you. Healthy associations can also help you develop new business opportunities and raise capital.

In the following chapters, we'll look at each of these principles in detail. During my years as a McDonald's owner, I rarely focused on money. Instead, I focused on the freedom I found by following these freedom concepts. Yet today, I have all the money I could ever need.

Living in freedom occurs when you get up in the morning and go to life, not to a job. You go to life and get paid for it. I've learned the hard way how to live in freedom. I've learned through the struggles of living without money and without the comforts of a home. I've learned through the struggles of becoming a McDonald's owner at a young age and learning on the job. I traveled through the arches, through entrepreneurship, and came out the other side a wealthy and free man. Now I want to pass along the knowledge I gained.

Entrepreneurship, when done right, is a wonderful adventure. Turn the page and let the adventure begin!

FAITH

TWO
Ground Zero of Business Success

In April 2001 I got into my car and drove away from Chicago to my new home in Michigan. Other than my four years of college, Chicago was all I had ever known. I had experienced many ups and downs there. I had lived through my parents' divorce, life on welfare, and many evictions as a child. I overcame those obstacles, graduated college, and enjoyed a successful career with several companies in the food industry. Now, however, I faced something completely different.

I merged onto the interstate and watched as my hometown faded in the rearview mirror. Thoughts of my family and friends consumed me and tears welled in my eyes. Throughout my life, the people I loved had always been nearby. Now I was alone and feeling out of my league. *Am I cut out to be a McDonald's owner? This is a mistake.* But something urged me on. I drove mile after mile on two things: the fuel in my car and the fuel in my heart. That fuel was faith. And at that moment, it was the only thing I had going for me.

In order to begin a book on entrepreneurship, I have to start where most books on the subject will not—with the essential principle for entrepreneurial freedom, the ground zero of business success. I have to begin with *faith*.

Since the Beginning of Time

As you drive into work on Monday morning, you know something's wrong. The rush-hour traffic crawls around you, but you pay no attention to it. You're antsy. Your mind is spinning, but you're not thinking about work. You walk into the office, the restaurant, the business, and you look around at the details of what your company does every day. One thought takes over: *I could do things better if I were in charge. I need to be my own boss.* You proceed through the day playing Monday-morning quarterback. Questioning everything. Seeing clearly how you could improve things or scrap things completely and start over. Your mind isn't on the task at hand. Your body is there, going through the motions, but your thoughts are designing the dreams of your future. What's happening to you?

You're having what author Michael Gerber called an *entrepreneurial seizure*.[1]

Many people experience an entrepreneurial seizure. We're all born with a desire to create and to build. In my opinion, everyone is born to be an entrepreneur. That's

---

1. Michael Gerber, *The E-Myth: Why Most Businesses Don't Work and What to Do About It* (Pensacola, FL: Ballinger Publishing Company, 1985).

why everyone—at one time or another—grows frustrated with his or her job. Our creative instincts conflict with the rules and structure of our employers.

In the Bible, the apostle Peter tells us that God's "divine power has given to us all things that pertain to life and godliness."[2] We have everything we need. We don't need to work in a passionless job, living for that future day when we can cash in our 401(k), and then start to live. We have been given everything we need for life—for living in freedom every day.

We can go back to the very beginning of time to see this is true. God created the universe, the earth, and human beings. When he created humans, he created them in his image. We were given the same spark of creativity that God used to create everything we know in the natural world.

Although God made us in his image, he made us in flesh so we could take care of business. After creating humans, "God blessed them, and God said to them, 'Be fruitful and multiply; fill the earth and subdue it.'"[3]

Be fruitful. Fill the earth. Subdue. We were not designed to be wallflowers. We were designed to be creative, to be expansive, and to conquer whatever obstacles may be placed in front of us. Entrepreneurship, at its core, was implanted in us at the beginning of time.

We are all made to be entrepreneurs, but not everyone is ready. So how do we know if we're ready or not?

To begin with, we need to have faith.

---

2. 2 Peter 1:3.
3. Genesis 1:28.

Faith is the most powerful tool in the universe.

The Bible tells about a woman who was healed by her faith.[4] Jesus was walking through a large crowd, and the people were pressing in on him, nearly crushing him. Among the crowd was a woman who had suffered from uncontrolled bleeding for twelve years. She had gone from doctor to doctor, but no one could heal her. She had placed her health in the hands of other people and come up empty. Then she saw Jesus, and knowing he was a great man, she tried to get near him. The people pressed in, so she couldn't get all the way to him. But she reached out and touched the edge of his cloak, believing even that could help her. Immediately, her bleeding stopped.

Jesus knew something had happened. "Who touched me?" he asked. "I know that power has gone out of me."

The woman fell, trembling, at his feet and told Jesus why she had touched his garment.

Jesus' cloak held no special powers, and Jesus himself did not heal the woman. He told her, "Daughter, your faith has healed you. Go in peace."

In several more stories in the gospels, the same two things happen: people are healed by an encounter with Jesus, and he tells them their faith made the healing possible.

Faith. What can't it do?

---

4. See Luke 8:42–48.

Faith Required

In addition to healing physical ailments, faith gives us the foundation to branch out on our own, to be independent, to be entrepreneurs.

St. Augustine said that "Faith is to believe what you do not see; the reward of this faith is to see what you believe." In *The 7 Habits of Highly Effective People*, Stephen Covey talks about beginning with the end in mind.[5] A successful entrepreneur begins with the end in mind and sets out with complete faith that he can accomplish that vision. He cannot rely on his mama or his friends to believe in his vision for him. That belief has to begin within the deepest part of his soul.

In March 2009 I was at my grandmother's funeral. It was an emotional time, and I thought a lot about my life with Granny and the years since I had left Chicago. During the funeral, I noticed that my Uncle Tyrone kept watching me. Afterward he pulled me aside.

"I'm sure your grandmother's very proud of you," my uncle said. "Can I ask you a question? Did you always know you were going to be successful?"

I thought for a moment. Then I leaned forward and said, "If I hadn't known, I never would have been successful." Being convinced of my future success and achieving that success were two things that could not be separated.

That's what we have to understand. If we don't believe

---
5. Stephen Covey, *The 7 Habits of Highly Effective People*, rev. ed. (New York: Free Press, 2004).

it's going to happen, then it's *not* going to happen. Guaranteed.

The biggest obstacle preventing people from venturing into entrepreneurship or achieving success is fear. Fear and all its children: doubt, worry, anxiety. If that woman from the Bible story had been afraid to reach out to Jesus, she would never have received healing. When creative people are afraid to reach out for their dreams, they never have a chance to receive the opportunities destined for them.

When we have faith, we remove our fear that we don't have enough, that we are not enough, and that obstacles will subdue us instead of the other way around.

In the movie *The Great Debaters*, Forest Whitaker plays a professor who develops a debate team at a black college. The debate team goes on to compete against and beat the Harvard debate team (the movie is based on a true story where the Wiley College debate team actually faced and beat the University of Southern California team—the best debaters at the time).

In one particularly poignant scene, the professor coaches his son and asks, "What is the thing that holds most people back?"

The son answers correctly. He doesn't say, "Knowledge." Instead, he says, "Fear and doubt."

The professor and his son knew that to achieve success as a debate team, the biggest obstacle they would face would not be their opponent, nor would it be the judge. Their biggest obstacle would be the fear and doubt that could weigh heavily within them and pull them down.

Fortunately, we already have what we need. The genesis of success already lies within us. Maybe you don't have all the knowledge you need, but you can go out and get that knowledge. The word *education* comes from the Latin word *educere*, which means "to draw out." So expanding our knowledge is just a way to draw out the abilities we already possess. It takes the principle that God "has given us everything we need for life" and gives it wings.

When we develop the right vision, understand our purpose, have a fire-in-the-belly passion, take ownership of our responsibilities and education, and develop healthy and productive associations, our innate ability to succeed will be drawn out of us.

On the surface, it may seem that faith and business are two separate things. Some people go to church on Sundays and go to work on Mondays, and they hold these two areas of their lives apart. But belief and business success are married together. Business success requires a belief in your self-worth, a belief in your unique talents, a belief that success is an inside job, and a belief that, in good times and in bad, you hold the power to live in freedom every day. We have to maximize our belief in those things, and I know only one way to do that: we must have a complete faith in God and his love for us.

The Bible says: "Without faith it is impossible to please God, because anyone who comes to him must believe that he exists and that he rewards those who earnestly seek him."[6] God exists, and he rewards those who seek him—that is the foundation of all entrepreneurial success. When I use the words *entrepreneurial success*, I mean business leaders who achieve balanced success in all areas of their entrepreneurial life—not just their lives spent in the office but also their lives spent with family, with friends, and in the community. To achieve true, complete entrepreneurial success, you must have faith in God and follow his lead.

Overcoming the Fear Freeze

When one of Jesus' followers failed to live up to his expectations, he sometimes would call them "Ye of little faith." He knew faith was the most powerful force in the universe, and he knew that its opposite, doubt, was equally powerful. That's why, if you're going to be an entrepreneur, before you choose your business, before you write a business plan, before you hire a CPA, or a lawyer, or a bookkeeper, you must have an unshakable ability to wrestle with, and ultimately defeat, fear.

Fear can be defined as False Expectations Appearing Real. It is an expectation of a future that God does not have in store for you. Since the beginning of creation, he has had something entirely better planned for your destiny. But fear is a temptation. Fear is playing it safe. Studies have shown that the thing you fear the most almost never comes to fruition. It's a product of your mind, a product of playing old tapes, of looking

---
6. Hebrews 11:6 (NIV).

Ground Zero of Business Success

backward. But we can "see" failure easier than we can "see" success, so it is easier to believe in it. This is a temptation we must resist at all costs.

Just like most temptations, we can't avoid fear completely. We must face it and overcome it. There were many times during my McDonald's ownership days when I was scared as hell. To be honest, I can't think of a major decision I made without being scared. But I had the courage to make the decision, and make it in a timely manner, and that made all the difference.

Fear freezes some people. They think, *If I can just avoid the situation, it will go away.* But in life, in living in freedom, there is no such thing as standing still. We are programmed to take a fight-or-flight approach to challenges. We either take the fight to the problem or we run away from it—by quitting or by sticking our head in the sand. But you're an entrepreneur. You're a fighter, a creator, a problem solver, so you must take the information you have, imperfect as it may be, and move forward in faith.

The famous World War II general, George Patton,

Freedom Thought

How strong is your faith? Do you find it easy to believe in yourself, or do fear and doubt tempt you too often? As a budding entrepreneur, you must remind yourself each day that you have everything you need for success. God has already given it to you!

To be a successful entrepreneur, faith is required. If I hadn't believed in my vision, I would have failed. You need to get up every day, look in the mirror, and banish fear and doubt. Embrace the good things God has ordained for you and believe!

said, "A good plan violently executed now is better than a perfect plan executed next week." What Patton meant by "violently" is obvious. He was a victorious general in the bloodiest of wars. But we could easily use "passionately executed" and the statement would apply to us. Faith gives us the courage to strike now for victory and not allow imperfect choices to paralyze us. Faith gives us the courage to not postpone our dreams for the fairy tale of some future time when the perfect circumstances materialize. That doesn't mean we should jump into a situation without preparing for it, but we can't allow the excuse of needing perfect circumstances keep us from venturing out.

You *will* be tempted by fear. But in Paul's first letter to the Corinthians, he says, "No temptation has seized you except what is common to man. And God is faithful; he will not let you be tempted beyond what you can bear. But when you are tempted, he will also provide a way out so that you can stand up under it."[7] You will face doubts and worries. I sure have. But God is faithful. He will always offer a way past the fear, and he will always give you what you need.

---

7. 1 Corinthians 10:13 (NIV).

THREE

The Journey of Creativity

When I arrived in Michigan to open my new stores, I had faith, a big vision, and plenty of passion, but not much more. At my first meeting with the McDonald's people in Michigan, they asked me, "Who's on your team?"

I didn't have a team. It was just me. I needed a CPA, a bookkeeper, a lawyer, and an assistant. But more than that, I needed employees. More than one hundred employees to be exact. I won't deny there was a part of me that still wanted to turn around and head for home—back to the comforts of Chicago.

In that way, I wasn't much different than the ancient Israelites after they escaped from Egypt. Following four hundred years of slavery, the challenges of freedom—of living in freedom every day—didn't come easy for the Israelites. They had to wander in the desert. They had to rely on an unseeable God instead of a seeable pharaoh. When it came time to enter the Promised Land, they chickened out. "Would it not be better for us to return to Egypt?" they wondered.[1]

---
1. Numbers 14:3.

They wanted to return to slavery!

They wanted to return to slavery because fear had filled them up and conquered them.

Entrepreneurship is filled with exhilarating mountaintop *and* challenging valley experiences. The mountains are easy. You're feeling good. You opened your store. Or you landed the major account. Or you got your first great review. Those experiences can carry you for a while, but not forever. You have to get through the inevitable valleys—the lost account, the poor month of sales—to get back to the next mountain.

One day during the lengthy process of hiring employees and managers, I came home to my townhouse, feeling defeated. I was alone (my wife and children had yet to move up from Chicago), and I buried my face in my hands and cried. The only person to talk to was God. "What have you done, Lord? Do you really think I'm worthy? I'm the steward of all these people."

I was in the valley. The mountain high I'd experienced when McDonald's approved the purchase of my stores had worn off. To get through the valley, I had to turn to the only one who could see me through. I had learned to seek the Lord's presence by watching my mother do the same thing when we were evicted from home after home. She would always come out of those bleak experiences with renewed conviction. "He didn't bring us this far to abandon us now," she would say.

I thought of my mother, and her words comforted

me. *He's not going to abandon me now. I just need to trust that he'll take care of things.*

The more I prayed, the more I felt God's presence. I went to work the next day with renewed faith. Although I couldn't understand how it was all going to unfold, I relied on my God and my vision of success. A year later, after a series of successes, I received the McDonald's Rookie Owner of the Year Award for the Michigan Region. I was firmly on the road of success.

You will experience dark days as a business owner. In business, as in life, you must go through some valleys to get to the mountains. Most people are familiar with the Twenty-third Psalm, which contains the reassuring line, "Even though I walk through the valley of the shadow of death, I will fear no evil, for you are with me."[2] I love that line because it says I'm "walking through" the valley. It doesn't say I'm "standing" or "living" in the valley. I'm traveling through, and I *will* come out on the other side. When you're firmly planted somewhere, you can't help but look around and see what surrounds you. Yet when you're going through something, you can focus on what you're *going to,* and not what you're *in* at the moment.

Create a Way

Within the shadow of the valley, it can look like there's no way out. But faith gives you the confidence you need to believe in a way, and if there is no existing way, then faith gives you the courage to create a way. Faith gives us a

---
2. Psalm 23:3–4 (NIV).

way to freedom. That is the essence of entrepreneurship: when there is no path, we have to create one. You take nothing and make it into something. You believe in things other people will tell you are impossible.

Creativity is necessary to be successful as an entrepreneur, and faith is necessary for creativity. You can't have one without the other.

I dealt with more than a few challenges while working within the McDonald's system. At times, my desire to do what I wanted bumped against the rules of the McDonald's way. And the rules of McDonald's bent about as well as the metal pole of a basketball hoop when you collide into it. Some owners are afraid of rules, afraid of making mistakes. However, faith gave me permission to make mistakes—to bump up against the system, take my lumps, and try again. Faith allowed me to make decisions quicker because I wasn't afraid of the repercussions. Faith helped me figure out what to change when I faced an apparent dead end.

Fear sees barriers that cannot be crossed. Faith sees not barriers but borders—borders that may be challenging to cross, but can be crossed nonetheless. To cross a border, you might need to ford a river or travel in a different direction to get across, but it won't stop anyone with enough belief in themselves.

Confidence in yourself and your vision redirects your thoughts toward creative solutions. Prescription antidepressants work in much the same way. When children grow up in abusive situations, they learn to use fear to their advantage. They stay away from dangerous situations the best way they can. But their brains eventually get hardwired to cling to fear and to continue avoiding risk. What worked well for them in childhood becomes an albatross in their adult years. Fear prevents them from taking chances and from fully exploring their God-given creativity. So a doctor might prescribe them an antidepressant. Such medications help rewire the brain to overcome the fear. Their thoughts are released from the mental barriers that imprison them. In the world of independent business, God serves as the antifear prescription that we all need.

As entrepreneurs, we will face the prospect of fearing two types of failures: event failure and ultimate failure. We cannot avoid event failure. Some things will not go right for us. But we can avoid ultimate failure. Ultimate failure only comes when we get knocked down by an event failure and we don't get back up.

Recently I spoke to a group of business students at Southern Illinois University at Carbondale. By then I had sold my stores for an enormous profit, and I had moved onto the next phase in my life, including coaching other aspiring entrepreneurs. During the question-and-answer session, a young man asked me a particularly interesting question. This man knew that not everything is perfect in the independent business world. "You've done a lot in your young life," he said. "Do you have any regrets? Surely, you must have some."

"No," was my immediate answer. I meant it. Regrets

come from making bad decisions. But with a strong belief in God, myself, my employees, and my customers, I just made decisions—they weren't bad; they weren't good; they were just decisions. I learned from the ones with poor results as much as I learned from the ones that worked well, and now I have a file cabinet of experiences to draw from during my next ventures and in coaching others. Those experiences are resources.

You're a Masterpiece

Certainty in your ultimate success gives you the freedom to prepare yourself for that outcome. You prepare yourself for a future that is not guaranteed, but one you believe in as if it *is* guaranteed. Then when the opportunity comes along, you're ready. You can identify it as an opportunity and pounce on it.

When we lack certainty, we feel as if the future needs to unfold exactly as we want it to. But belief in ourselves and our future allows God to unfold our future in unexpected, and often, more beneficial ways. My original dream was to open up my own restaurant—Ken's Hot Dog Stands. I never envisioned owning a McDonald's, let alone two. But when the opportunity presented itself, I was ready. I had been in the game, mixing it up, interacting with people, trying new things, learning new things. When the time was right, something far better than a hot dog stand had come along.

God has a plan for each of our lives. It is ordained, like a destination that is unseen over the horizon. But we have to work out that plan. Each McDonald's store has a unique number assigned to it. They get the number when they are completed and opened for the first time. I owned two stores—one that existed and one that was built. The newly built store was #24733. The other store was #1252. It had existed for a long time, but I was destined to own it. I had a vision to own a restaurant, and faith in that vision, and then I made choices along the way to get there. I had to put on some work clothes and make it happen. The people I met along the way, the places I came to, the situations I faced—they all worked to fulfill my destiny of owning #1252—something God had ordained long before I came along. And now that I've retired from McDonald's, I'm putting on new work clothes. With faith in my next destiny, I'm walking out to a new future where I can help other people achieve their dreams.

Work and belief go hand in hand. Belief gives you the tenacity to stick to goals. You don't have to depend on other people to motivate you. Likewise, you're not as vulnerable to the naysayers. You seek your motivation from a higher power than the friends who never made it out of the hood, the friends who might be jealous of your potential. Belief gives you the conviction of heart that, in the end, you will not ultimately fail. You may "event fail" your way to success—hitting bumps in the road, taking detours, evolving your plan—but in the end, you will persevere.

Later, I will go into detail on my *people first, not profits* philosophy. But for now, let me just say that I sometimes went to extreme lengths to put my employees and customers first. I paid my employees far above the typical rate, and I added levels of service rarely seen within a McDonald's restaurant. I was sometimes ridiculed for taking such measures. One owner openly laughed at me. Other owners and some people within corporate McDonald's predicted my failure. "This is a business, not a charity. You're not some government aid agency. You're going to go bankrupt."

I disagreed. I was in my creative zone. Yes, I needed to learn about managing a budget. Yes, I got myself in financial trouble a few times in the beginning. But my philosophy about people was a required part of my success strategy, and it worked. I had to believe in it and in myself.

My job was to have faith in myself and then "do me"—to play to my strengths. Each of us is "wonderfully made."[3] Each of us is an original, a masterpiece; we have no competition. In business, I didn't have any competition. My competition wasn't the Wendy's down the street. My only competition was me. Nobody could beat me at being me. I was the only one who held the power to prevent my ultimate success. If I didn't use doubt and fear to compete against myself, if instead I had faith in myself, then my ultimate success was guaranteed.

Robert Kennedy once famously used a line from a play by George Bernard Shaw: "There are those that

---
3. Psalm 139:14.

look at things the way they are and ask, 'Why?' I dream of things that never were and ask, 'Why not?'" That to me says entrepreneurship. That says freedom. That says faith. The faith to see things differently. The faith to find a need and fill it. The faith to challenge the system within the spirit of improvement.

Mind Map out of Failure

When I'm coaching someone about fear, I emphasize that fear is a thought. It's vapor; it's not real. Then I have him or her do something I call a mind map. We walk through the thoughts. We talk about the problems, all the possible scenarios, and the alternatives—the solutions and strategies. Almost always, when we finish talking, the person realizes two things. First, that the prospects are much better than his or her mind initially conceived. And, second, even if things don't work out, the failure is only an event failure. For someone with faith, there are limitless ways to bounce back.

I overcame my initial fears when I moved to Michigan and opened the stores. I was able to step up to the next level, but new levels bring new devils. A few years into my tenure as a McDonald's owner, I still wasn't financially savvy. I was focused on developing a system of exceptional customer service. I was doing some unorthodox things, stretching the conformity limits of the McDonald's system, and trying to create something different. In the process, I ran out of capital a couple of times. Money was coming in—sales were going up—but money was going right back out the door again. I didn't have any in the bank.

To make matters worse, I got behind in my taxes—$200,000 behind, to be exact. My vision was bigger than my pocketbook, and I didn't have the financial knowledge to keep up with it.

McDonald's started making noises about taking away my franchise rights, and I had nightmares about arriving at my stores in the morning and finding the doors chained and locked. For a while, I focused on the things I didn't have. I didn't have money and I didn't have adequate financial knowledge. For a few days, it paralyzed me. The weight of the burden overpowered me. I couldn't sleep. I was embarrassed and afraid to share my problems with anyone.

That is the point where many people fold. That is the point where many people convert their event failure into an ultimate failure. But one morning, I didn't go immediately into work. I went to a park instead and did a mind map on myself. I walked through the alternatives, and instead of focusing on what I didn't have, I made a mental list of what I did have. I had energy. I had vision. I had increased sales. I had relationships with knowledgeable people who could advise me if I was willing to be vulnerable and approach them. I had a lot going for me. Because of my faith, I summoned the courage to talk with people who were financially savvy. Eventually, through better money management, I dug myself out of the situation. I learned from my event failure, and I didn't let that same thing happen again. I failed my way to success.

In owning a business and being an entrepreneur, you will have to persevere. There will be great moments where passion and adrenaline carry you through. But there will be tough moments where you will have to "stick with it."

You'll have to do and learn things you don't want to do and learn. Albert E. N. Gray, in a famous message written for life insurance professionals in 1940, said, "The successful person has the habit of doing the things failures don't like to do . . . [Successful people] don't like doing them either necessarily. But their disliking is subordinated to the strength of their purpose."

There's an old saying that goes, "You've got to fake it until you make it." Not everyone likes that statement. They think it means you should not be real; you should be inauthentic. I see the adage differently, however, and try to follow it. To me it means acting with courage. While I was a McDonald's owner, there was rarely a day where I didn't face some fear. But I had to act in spite of that

> **Freedom Thought**
>
> *Take a moment and do a mind map on yourself. List all the things you have going for you (your experiences, your knowledge, your visions of success, the smart and supportive people you know, the love of a God who has planned great things for you, etc).*
>
> *Your days as an entrepreneur will bring enjoyable mountaintop experiences and difficult valleys to travel through. To get through the valleys, you will need courage and creativity. With faith in everything you have going for you, you will take chances, break down barriers, and discover entrepreneurial freedom.*

fear. So many people depended on me, I couldn't walk around giving off nonbelieving vibes. I had to project confidence even when I wasn't completely feeling it. It's bad enough when business owners don't have adequate faith in success, but when their employees, customers, and vendors don't have confidence, then success becomes impossible.

Success is a journey, not a destination. Failure is never fatal and success is never final. I've known too many people—friends and family, business colleagues, coaching clients—who have made one big mistake, and then camped for the rest of their life. They didn't quit, but they didn't keep pushing upward. They stopped trying to improve their business or improve themselves. They didn't develop an exit strategy and didn't explore new opportunities along the journey. In business (as in life) you have quitters, campers, and climbers. In order to climb, you must have faith to propel you upward—upward to the pinnacle of your current venture, and then upward further to the next opportunity.

Entrepreneurial freedom is not a place where we rest on what we have done in the past. True entrepreneurial freedom is movement. Always improving, always moving toward the next opportunity. With faith, we can achieve our dreams—and more.

FOUR
Working It

Historically black colleges were founded to serve the unmet needs of black students. The schools believed in the success potential of all their students, and their results proved their faith was well placed. Historically black colleges turned out successful black graduates in numbers never seen before. In 1905, for example, Tuskegee Institute produced more self-made millionaires than Harvard, Yale, and Princeton combined. The schools graduated future CEOs, inventors, and politicians. Graduates like Booker T. Washington and Dr. Martin Luther King Jr. reached new heights in terms of success.

The schools also recognized that although we inhabit human bodies, we are actually spiritual beings. Our odds of achieving success are significantly higher when we embrace this fact. Historically black colleges taught core classes specific to a particular field of study, but they also taught theology and biblical principles. They recognized that each of their students was a spiritual being, and they needed a holistic view of the world. They believed a student leaving college could not separate faith from success. They worked to build the faith of their graduates.

If your faith is weak, there are things you can do to build it up. Faith is like a muscle. Just as muscles are developed through regular exercise, a life with God is something you build through discipline and habits. You have to exercise it to grow it, and you have to keep exercising to maintain it. You have to work your faith.

Renewing Your Mind

In his letter to the Romans, Paul wrote, "Do not be conformed to this world, but be transformed by the renewing of your mind."[1] That's what it takes to keep the world from limiting you—to keep the normal, dull way people conduct business from limiting you.

The time we spend transforming our minds acts as a seed planted in our hearts. The seed stays with us and grows. When we train ourselves to seek God throughout the day, we tap into his power and the creative force that runs through us. Our thoughts flow freely. We stay focused on everything we are blessed with instead of fixating on our problems in such a way that makes them seem unsolvable.

Recently I watched a movie I had seen before. The film came to a scene I didn't like, so I quickly grabbed the remote and fast-forwarded through it. But we can't do that with the negative thoughts we replay in our minds. We can't stick with the same thoughts if they're

1. Romans 12:2.

not working for us, nor can we skip over them. As with a bad movie, we have to get off the couch, hit eject, and put in something new. That's called renewing your mind. That's called taking control of your thoughts and giving yourself a new script.

Renewing your mind gives you a defense against conformity and self-doubt. There will always be detractors if you try to do something original. In business ownership, you'll find that advisors, CPAs, and even friends and family will discourage you from going against the grain. In my case, in a franchise setting, I faced enormous pressure to conform in every way to the McDonald's system. Without renewing my mind every day, I couldn't have pushed the envelope of the system and done things rarely done within McDonald's—things that were keys to my success.

The habit of mind renewal begins with setting aside time every day to be with God. We can be with God in three ways—praying, reading Scripture, and reading a daily devotion.

Our prayer time should begin first thing in the morning—before we do anything else, and certainly before we talk with anyone else or check e-mail. We should find a quiet place and have a spiritual conversation with God. Sometimes having a conversation means that we do the talking—tell God what we're dealing with and what we need. Other times, it means listening. The conversation goes both ways, and although most people don't hear God's voice audibly, when we develop our prayer habit, we'll "hear" him in a spiritual way.

During that morning time, we also need to read. Some people might not like reading, or they might think they're not good at it. But again, spiritual reading is just another muscle that needs to be exercised. You have to begin and stick with it. The most important thing we need to read is the Bible. What we read on is what we feed on, and the Bible is God's Word, providing the universal truths we need to succeed. It is there we find and understand the plan God has for us.

I've spent a lot of time memorizing verses from the Bible. People say I often speak in sound bites, and if you've attended one of my speaking engagements, you would probably agree. I quote Scripture verses and the words of influential people. These words serve as a rope of hope for me, and I can't help but share them. They are a foundation to rely on when times get tough or when I need to seek direction to overcome an obstacle. In the Bible, I read a chapter every day from the book of Proverbs. There are thirty-one chapters, so that gives me one chapter per day of the month. I also read from the New Testament and the Psalms. In addition, I read from a daily devotional book. For example, I am currently reading *Jesus Calling: Enjoying Peace in His Presence* by Sarah Young. Some of my other favorite devotional books have been *Starting Your Day Right* and *Ending Your Day Right* by Joyce Meyer, *TGIF: Today God Is First* by Os Hillman, and *My Utmost for His Highest* by Oswald Chambers.

I can't express how crucial this reading program is to my success as an entrepreneur. Without a doubt, I *would not* have achieved the things I did without spending my first hour this way. But for me, it didn't stop with that first morning hour. I have devotional books in every room of my house and at my office. I often take five or ten minutes during various times of the day to reconnect with the source of my life and my creativity.

When we read about Jesus, we see how much he gave of himself. Everyone wanted something from him, and he gave of himself energetically. He gave his healing touch, he gave his wisdom, and he gave his love. But what else did he do? He always found time to get away and be alone with his Father. He unplugged from the world and plugged into the Source. That's the model we have to follow.

As an entrepreneur, you have to keep many plates in the air. You have your business, your customers, your employees, your family, and your friends. People want things from you, and you have to provide. In order to sustain your energy and creativity, you have to plug into the Source at least once a day, if not more.

You can also renew your mind by having the faith to introduce yourself to new experiences. In order to have things you've never had before, you have to be willing to do some things you've never done before. You must believe in your ability to learn. I wasn't the smartest kid in the world. I took the ACT college-entry test three times. I got a 15 the first time, a 16 the second, and a

17 the third. That's out of a total possible score of 36. But what I lacked in book education, I replaced with a determination to gain real-world knowledge.

Walking in faith requires that you embrace every opportunity to learn new things relevant to your vision. Despite my ACT scores, I went to college and learned a lot. It benefited me immensely. But college didn't prepare me to become an entrepreneur; it prepared me to get a job. To prepare for business ownership, I needed experience, even when that experience didn't fit within a normal career path.

If you've read my first book, *A Leap of Faith*, you might recall the many jobs (what I called *paid internships*) I took to expand my knowledge of the food industry. For example, I had spent many years working in the food supplier side of the business, but when an unexpected opportunity came up to wait on tables at a high-end restaurant, I took it. I had concerns about my ability to be successful as a waiter. I had always been clumsy. I could barely jump over a box of Cracker Jacks. My equilibrium had always been off. I was afraid I would drop a full tray of plates on top of my customers. But I decided to overcome those fears and fake it until I made it.

Faith is jumping off the top of the tallest building and growing your wings on the way down. So I took a leap of faith and learned to serve tables in a high-end environment. I became proficient, and eventually I became the favorite server of two regulars, Edie and Eric Waddell. Edie was an executive with McDonald's, and through a series of events, she eventually paved the way for me to become an owner.

There's an old Buddhist proverb that says: "When the student is ready, the teacher will appear." A "teacher" can be anything (person or situation) that gives us new knowledge and skills. For me, Edie came along when I was ready and taught me about the world of McDonald's.

Being the Light

There's a reason why customer service is at such an all-time low. People are sitting on the sidelines of life, working a job they hate, piling up their 401(k) for a day when their lives are nearly over. They lack the energy and creativity to make their customers happy. Fear kills the spirit—the entrepreneur's spirit—within all of us.

Faith, however, produces joy. And joy is contagious.

I don't seek happiness. I seek joy. Happiness depends on what's happening around you. It's attached to a situation—a person, place, or thing. Joy, on the other hand, comes from somewhere deeper. It comes from an unbreakable faith. When you have joy, people will notice. They will say, "There's something different about you." You'll be known as someone who always gives his or her best—someone who loves and respects others, someone who operates with integrity. And that's important. Not only will that benefit other people but also your business.

There's a lot of chatter these days about corporate responsibility—treating employees well, protecting the environment, and creating a diverse workplace. Companies want to be perceived as doing the right thing. But too often, we hear stories about Enron and Bernie Madoff—businesses and businesspeople who sacrificed integrity at the altar of self-interest and greed. When we stay close to God, however, when we believe in ourselves and our business, it's easier to make the right choices. It's easier to spread that light throughout our business.

As a business leader, I saw my "job" as shining a light into the world. That didn't mean I beat people over the head with Scripture. Sometimes Christian business leaders go around quoting Scripture and scaring people. Jesus never did that. He met people where they were. He talked to fishermen and told them to cast their nets on the other side. He talked to farmers and told them about planting seeds. Jesus was himself. Jesus wasn't a Christian; Jesus was Jesus.

When I say "shining the light into the world," I'm not necessarily talking about religion and going to church every week. Those are good things, and everyone has to find his or her own way regarding them. I'm talking instead about wearing your faith and taking it to work, 365. It's about being an ambassador to the world—helping people and talking with them on their terms. Too many Christians get focused on doing business with other Christians. That's the wrong approach. As owners, we're in a position of influence, and we need to use our faith to make the world a better place for everyone—especially people who might not be living peaceful lives.

I don't care where I am, I pray before each meal. My family prays before each meal, but I also pray before a lunch meeting. I even prayed when eating at one of my restaurants. I don't force it on anyone else, but when I bend my head, something happens. People get quiet. All eyes are on me like the last slice of pie. There's an innate desire to respect someone's act of prayer, and I know that not hiding my faith encourages some people to explore theirs.

People are hungry for a sense of purpose, and your faith can help them find that purpose. Many people are open to faith-based conversations. In 2007 the Wharton School of the University of Pennsylvania identified the inclusion of religion as an emerging trend in the business world. To quote from an article that appeared in CNN.com about the study:

> "The old paradigm of leaving your beliefs behind when you go to work is no longer satisfying," said Stew Friedman, practice professor of management at Wharton and director of the school's Work/Life Integration Project.
>
> "More than ever, people want work that fits in with a larger sense of purpose in life. For many people, that includes a concept of God, or something like it."[2]

---

2. Peter Walker, "Balancing Faith and Business," CNN.com, February 12, 2007, http://edition.cnn.com/2007/BUSINESS/01/31/execed.religion/index.html,

When you're the light to other people, word gets around. One highlight of my McDonald's ownership career was when I was profiled in a magazine article titled, "The Lifestyles of the Rich and Faithful."[3] It described how I was able to become a McDonald's owner and achieve success without compromising my faith. I was proud of that article because I knew it meant I had achieved true success.

Giving Back

Tithing is another practice Christians often participate in. For example, many people give 10 percent of their gross income to their church—to the work of God in the world. That's a personal decision, obviously, but I also believe tithing out of your business is a key to success. It's another act of faith.

There are rules of engagement for everything around us. There were rules of engagement in the McDonald's system. They had a system figured out, and if you adhered to that system, things usually worked in your favor. Sometimes I tried to stretch the system, but I never abandoned it. Likewise, I believe tithing is a system, and not just a biblical system; it's a universal system. You reap what you sow. If you sow sparingly, you reap sparingly. If you sow abundantly, you meet with success. It's a system with its own rules of engagement.

---

3. Nicolla Price, "The Lifestyles of the Rich and Faithful," *Inspired Living*, Winter/Spring 2006.

Working It

> **Freedom Thought**
>
> Developing your faith takes discipline. Now is the time to develop that discipline. Set aside time with God each day—preferably first thing in the morning. Also, set aside time to read the Bible and devotionals.
>
> We must continually renew our minds. Until we develop our faith habits, it's helpful to develop a specific schedule for those practices and to record that schedule in our daily calendars.
>
> By developing a "renewing your mind" discipline, you can develop the faith needed for success, and you can be a light to the world.

In tithing, you take 10 percent of your business's gross income and use it to make an impact in the community. It's a way of recognizing that God played a role in your success. It's a way of recognizing that other people in your community—family, friends, business associates, customers, employees, vendors—played a role in your success. Nobody accomplishes anything significant alone. You take 10 percent off the top, and you say thank you.

It's a matter of priorities. When I cut checks to my employees, the government has already come in and taken out its share. On the tenth of every month, I had to pay McDonald's a fee based on my sales. Businesspeople take home their profits and dump a large percentage into stocks or real estate investments. People and businesses "tithe" all the time. But they don't always have their priorities in the proper order—they tithe to the government or to their personal wealth. By giving to others first, we enable people, including ourselves, to be blessed. God tells us to give our tithes "and see if I will not throw open the floodgates of heaven and pour out so much blessing that you will not have room enough for it."[4]

I consider tithing such a critical principle that I will not waver from it. When I sold my first store, I wrote a check to a single church for more than $100,000. My CPA went crazy. "See here, Ken," he said, "I can understand your need to be philanthropic—"

"It's not being philanthropic," I told him, "it's a principle."

"Okay, but why don't we do it over a period of time? We can pay a quarter of it this year, a quarter next year, and so on."

"No. Pay it all now. It doesn't belong to me."

"But it does belong to you. You earned it. Your sales have been phenomenal."

"They've been phenomenal because I adhered to this principle."

Tithing is a system that keeps things flowing. It's reciprocity. And it keeps me humble. It reminds me that, while it is up to me, it's not about me. If I help take care of others, then I will be taken care of also.

I believe giving a tithe to a church is a good idea. Churches are connected to the community, and they operate many programs that make a significant impact in people's lives. They're connected with people who don't have money for food and water. At McDonald's, we threw away food every day. Everywhere today, people walk around drinking bottled water, taking that clean

---

4. Malachi 3:10.

fresh water for granted. I have to pay back into the system.

You don't have to give to a church. There are many good charities available. After I sold my second store, I set up a scholarship fund at my alma mater, Southern Illinois University at Carbondale. That fund will live for a long time and will help send a lot of people to college.

I'm paying back into the system and trying to be the light. Having faith is required for business success, but a complete faith doesn't stop with us. A complete faith spreads to other people so they can move forward with their lives and eventually reach their own ultimate success.

VISION

FIVE
The Glorious Image in Their Heads

When Andy was in college, he worked at the university bookstore. The store sold textbooks, college apparel, and some other items, like music CDs and other books for personal use. He was in business school, and while working, he spent a lot of time thinking about his future as a businessman. He tried to picture what it would look like.

As time went on, he formulated a vision in his mind. He wanted to be his own boss. He liked living in the college environment, but he realized that students didn't have a fun, hip place to buy their music and nonacademic books. They had to go into the university-owned store, which had a large, impersonal feel, or they had to drive ten miles to the chain bookstore at the nearest mall. Andy developed a vision of an intimate music and bookstore along the main street of the college town. He saw the eclectic rows of CDs and books. He saw the reading chairs and the hang-out tables. He saw the coffee bar. He saw a need, and he saw how to respond to it.

The vision infused Andy with energy and motivation, and he couldn't wait to get started. But after he graduated, he didn't write a business plan and lease a storefront property. He wanted to get his vision right, so he was patient. Although he could have landed a much higher paying position, he took a job as an entry-level sales clerk at a large bookstore. He found a small apartment, kept his expenses to a minimum, and saved his money.

He mastered that job, and within eighteen months, he worked his way into management. He learned general bookkeeping, inventory management, and marketing. While he learned, he kept thinking about his vision. The dream of opening his own store was his destination at the end of the horizon, and everything he did contributed to eventually realizing that dream. He targeted three college towns where he could picture himself living (there's that vision thing again). He would read the local newspapers, and he would spend his off-hours visiting the existing stores and even getting to know some of the owners. He developed a picture of what it would be like to own a store in those places, and that reaffirmed his vision even more.

After five years of working at two different bookstores, a storefront became available in one of the towns. It was time, right? Andy bought the store with his saved money and the rest is history, right? Well, not exactly.

The rent was affordable, and Andy was very interested. But the store was a block off the main street. It had a narrow shape, and he couldn't quite figure out how to arrange all the shelves and furniture he pictured in his vision. *Maybe I can get started here,* he thought, *then move to a better location in a few years.* He struggled for a few weeks about what to do, but in the end he decided to pass. The location fell too far short of his vision.

Andy redoubled his efforts. He spent the next month writing a business plan—putting all his experience to good use. If the right location became available, and he needed to pursue a loan, he would be ready. That opportunity came six months later when a local store owner, a man Andy had befriended during his visits to the town, decided to close his shop. A few months after that, Andy unlocked his door and welcomed his first customer to the manifestation of his vision.

He Shoots! He Scores!

When I'm hired as a coach for business owners, one of my first requests is to see their vision statement. Experience has taught me that when a business is struggling, usually it's lacking vision. Ralph Waldo Emerson said, "The world makes way for the man who knows where he's going." That speaks to freedom. That speaks to the power of vision. Emerson didn't say the world makes way "for the man who has detailed financial knowledge," or "for a man who found a great deal on rent," or even "for a man with a great work ethic." All those things will help you become successful. But the world making way for you? The world taking notice of you? That comes from knowing where you're going.

Business owners must know where they're going and where their business is going.

Far too many entrepreneurs don't do that, however. They get the cart before the horse. Go to any MBA school and you'll find the emphasis on developing a business plan. You know, the four Ps—product, price, promotion, and place—and all that. A business plan is an essential tool for starting and growing a business, but as we can see with Andy's experience, it comes after a vision is developed. In order to be successful entrepreneurs, we must develop our faith, and let that faith spill into a vision of where we want to go. To borrow one of Stephen Covey's seven habits of highly effective people, successful entrepreneurs "begin with the end in mind."[1] They apply their creative energy toward developing a picture of what success looks like to them.

I love to watch sports—basketball, football, golf, the Olympics—I love them all. I enjoy witnessing the drama as people of great skill work passionately to achieve their dreams. Yet I enjoy the interviews that take place afterward as much as the game or the event. A basketball player takes control at the end of a game, scoring seven points in the final minute, including a three-pointer at the buzzer for the win. A reporter approaches him on the floor and asks, "What were you thinking when the game was on the line? How did you come back? How were you able to beat the odds?"

---

1. Covey, *7 Habits of Highly Effective People*.

The Glorious Image in Their Heads

The player usually talks about faith. "I had no doubt we could do it. Those are the situations we prepare for." Sometimes he'll give you a glimpse into another secret of their success: "I saw myself making the shot."

We see this with many athletes, such as track-and-field runners. When they're warming up behind the starting line before a race, most of us know what's going through their minds. They're visualizing the race. They're envisioning success.

To understand the success of athletes, we have to start with the faith and vision pieces—not the detailed plans of their training (the sports equivalent of a business plan). I look at professional athletes as entrepreneurs of their own businesses. They begin with faith in themselves and a vision of what success looks like, then they wrap the details of success (i.e., training) around that. They use their faith to lock into the glorious image in their heads. They're like Tom Cruise in *Top Gun* using his radar to hone in on the enemy aircraft. Once he locks on that image of the aircraft and presses that red button, no matter how fast, how high, or how low that plane is flying, it's going down.

For most athletes, their vision began in childhood. They saw themselves taking the shot: "He shoots! He scores!" They saw themselves standing on the podium, "The Star-Spangled Banner" playing as the American flag was raised. At first the visions were just small sparks. But then the sparks grew into flames, and they saw more of the details. They saw their technique. They saw their body development. They saw the elements of the game or the race. They saw success.

Looking at the Mountain

In my previous book, *LIFE: Living in Freedom Everyday*, I told the story of Walt Disney and the creation of Space Mountain at Disneyland, but it's such a good story, it's worth retelling here.[2]

One day during the early days of Walt Disney World, Walt Disney was sitting on a bench at the amusement park. A worker spotted him staring into space and asked him what he was doing.

Disney replied, "I'm looking at my mountain."

There was no mountain where he looked—only empty space and empty grass—but Disney saw something nobody else could see. He had a vision. He passed along that vision to his employees and ordered the mountain to be built.

Of course, since then, millions of us have seen the mountain—Space Mountain—one of the most famous roller coasters in the world.

Unfortunately, Walt Disney died before construction of the attraction could be completed. Later, his widow, Lillian Disney, attended the opening ceremony. A Disney official, speaking before Mrs. Disney, celebrated the vision of Walt Disney but also lamented the fact that he didn't live to see his vision.

Mrs. Disney then came to the podium and had to correct

---

2. I originally read this story in Dr. Myles Munroe's book, *The Principles and Power of Vision* (New Kensington, PA: Whitaker House, 2006).

The Glorious Image in Their Heads

the official. "Walt already saw the mountain. It is you who are just now seeing it." She knew the mountain had been real to her husband from the first day he "saw it."

Walt Disney symbolized how to develop a vision. He was skilled at envisioning his dreams and making them happen, so it might have taken just an hour to come up with the Space Mountain idea. Still, he didn't do it while racing around managing his business empire. He did it while sitting on a bench and staring into space. He took quiet time for the essential act of visualizing.

I don't know the details of how Disney's vision unfolded during that time on the bench, but I'm guessing it didn't happen in an instant. Maybe he started thinking about a roller coaster. Then maybe he thought about an indoor roller coaster. Then maybe he thought about various structures that could house the roller coaster. At some point, the idea of a mountain developed within his imagination, and then finally, the image of a space-age-looking mountain.

Most successful entrepreneurs will tell you their success journey began with a vision. It probably began as a glimmer, a little spark of a concept, but with much chewing on it, with much daydreaming, it grew and grew.

As I mentioned in the previous section, my vision was to own a restaurant. It started out as a vision of Ken's Hot Dog Stands, but then the vision grew. As my career developed, it grew through various iterations until it became a detailed image of a successful McDonald's business.

Today, the entrepreneurial part of my vision is continuing to grow. My current vision is to take my knowledge of successful entrepreneurship and transform the lives of 4 million people. I'm aware that's a very ambitious vision, but that's the image that has developed in my mind, and I'm locking onto it.

Having a clear destination in my mind allows me to make intelligent decisions about my future actions. Do I want to run another restaurant? No. Do I want to open a store selling the latest and greatest products? No. Those are both wonderful ventures, but they don't conform to my current vision. Do I want to develop coaching and other advisory services that help people improve their lives and pursue success? Definitely. So the personal and business decisions I make must align with that, just as Andy's did when he made decisions (both in choosing to do things and choosing not to do things) that worked toward his vision.

Seeing the Impossibilities

One of my favorite quotes (attributed to several people, including, again, Ralph Waldo Emerson) says, "Do not follow where the path may lead. Go, instead, where there is no path and leave a trail." That's what vision does for you. It allows you to dream big, to dream about all the possibilities (and all the supposed impossibilities). Then you spend time leveraging and developing your talents and resources toward your goal.

We develop entrepreneurial vision when we focus on

the needs of people and try to find a way to meet those needs. America was built on the backs of entrepreneurs who discovered needs and dreamed big. People like Thomas Edison, Alexander Graham Bell, and Henry Ford changed this country, but they changed it by answering fundamental needs—needs such as improved access to communication and transportation. All the conveniences and luxuries we enjoy today were birthed at some point from entrepreneurship.

Edison and Bell were amazing men for their inventive genius, but I also like Henry Ford's story. Ford didn't invent the automobile (that's usually credited to Karl Benz). But Ford took an existing product and made it accessible to the general public. He married a product to a need for affordable, reliable transportation. He focused on efficient manufacturing and effective marketing, and his idea exploded across the country.

Life is about bold action and bold dreams. Life is not a series of straight paths we take to reach a status quo goal. You may decide that you want

Freedom Thought

What is your vision of success? What is your vision of your business? It's important for aspiring and current entrepreneurs to spend time developing their vision. Successful entrepreneurs "begin with the end in mind."

They are like athletes, preparing for the race and envisioning success. After reading this chapter, begin to develop a habit of picturing your future.

Spend time by yourself in a quiet place. Breathe deeply and relax. Let the images of success develop in your mind. Then keep repeating the process, enhancing your vision as you pursue and achieve your dream.

to work a crummy job for thirty years and collect your 401(k) so you can retire to the golf course, but that's not life. That's not living in freedom. That's coloring within the lines. That's hospice care—nursing care dedicated to easing the suffering of people who are dying. Life is about coloring outside the lines.

When I was in kindergarten, my mother got this message from my teacher: "Kenny's a very nice boy. He's very polite and well-behaved. But I can't get him to color inside the lines. He just won't do it." Apparently, I would color all over my papers, making quite a creative mess of things. My teacher probably saw it as a problem with following directions, but looking back, I see it as the beginning of my entrepreneurial career. I was seeing something that needed to be colored—something else that nobody else was seeing.

I don't think my teacher's concern bothered my mother much. My mother had a saying: "You can't be what you can't see." She believed in possibilities more than anyone I've ever known.

Although we faced many evictions during my childhood years, my mother, Mu'dear we called her, would always try to find us a nice, comfortable home to live in. Unfortunately, that would strain her finances. It would've been much easier financially if she had moved us to the projects. A friend of hers who lived in the projects would put pressure on her to move there, but Mu'dear refused.

Mu'dear also kept me in private school. And every

The Glorious Image in Their Heads

month after we picked up our welfare money from the Currency Exchange, we would stop for a treat on the way home. Usually we would stop at McDonald's, but sometimes she would take us to a fancy restaurant called the Millionaire's Club. We wouldn't order much—maybe a snack and a drink—but it gave us a chance to look over the fence. All of those things—the homes, private school, and the Millionaire's Club—could be considered controversial. But she wanted us to see the possibilities.

It worked. Despite great family struggles, I grew up thinking anything was possible. I had seen it and could picture it.

Now, many years later, I've proven it.

Once I was little Kenny from the block, little Kenny walking down the streets with my clothes in a bag, heading for the next place where my family would lay their heads. Now I'm a college graduate. Now I'm a multimillionaire. That happened because my mother taught me that I couldn't be what I couldn't see, and I believed her. I have always developed a vision for my future, and I have pursued it.

I saw my mountain and made it real.

SIX
Staying Out of the Ditch

As I progressed through the McDonald's system toward becoming an owner, I thought about what I would want my store to look like. I thought about it, and I pictured it.

When some business owners think about their business, they think about it only from their perspective: *What will my day look like when I'm an owner? How much money will I make? How will I manage my people?*

But I pictured my business from the customer's perspective. I knew I wanted my store to be an outstanding restaurant operation from their point of view. I knew I wanted my store to be a role model for other restaurants—a place that other owners could look to as an example. So before I had acquired the money or the buildings, I wrote down this vision statement for my future stores: "We will be a role model for what an outstanding restaurant operation should be." That was the central focus—succinct and clear. Then I added, "We will be known for our outstanding *quality, service,* and *cleanliness.*"

The purpose of the statement was to provide a vision for making our customers happy. You'll notice that it said nothing about profit. And it didn't say, "We will follow the business plan."

After I purchased the stores, I created a logo and went to Kinko's to make large signs of the logo and vision statement. I included the statement in the front of my employee handbook and trained every employee on it. I posted the signs in my restaurants so all employees could see it every day. If an employee's uniform wasn't neat and clean, or if they weren't polite to a customer, I didn't have to pull him into my office and berate him. I could simply walk over and point to the statement and say, "Read the vision."

Leadership and Swag

When we're driving and take our eyes off the road, bad things happen. When we're driving our dream and take our eyes off the vision, we drive into the ditch of failure. A lot of business owners spend time working on their business plan, working on their financing, but they don't put enough effort into their vision. When I conduct leadership training for various businesses, I always ask to see the vision statement. Sometimes they don't have one, and often, if they do, they can't put their hands on it. Or they might have had a vision statement written down somewhere—maybe it's on some plaque in the lobby or some obscure sheet of paper—but the employees rarely know what it is. As a result, the workers running the company are not aligned behind the vision of the leadership.

Most employees want to be led, but businesses fail them by not leading them toward a destination. They lead them in the tasks of the day, but nothing more. And because those tasks are not always aligned with the vision, the employees ultimately end up being inefficient and ineffective. Lorraine Monroe, author and education consultant, said, "The job of a good leader is to articulate a vision that others are inspired to follow. . . . Leadership is about making vision happen."

Profit objectives are not part of a leadership plan. Some business owners might assign a dollar figure to success (for example: "I'll consider myself a success if I earn $10,000 per year in profits."). But money is a by-product of success. It's not a goal. And it's not a vision.

Money may not be a vision, but you *can* tell business owners' priorities by where they put their money. Take a peek at their checkbook, and it will tell you whether they have a vision or not. Jesus told his disciples, "For where your treasure is, there your heart will be also."[1] If your heart is on your customers, that's where your money will be. If your heart is on your employees, that's where you money will be. If your heart is on your vision, that's where your money will be.

Eventually, a visionless business will fail in some way. The Bible says, "Where there is no vision, the people perish."[2] We can carry over this blunt proverb to

1. Matthew 6:21.
2. Proverbs 29:18 (KJV).

the survival possibilities of a business. Where there is no vision, the business will perish. If the business doesn't have any life, then it functions on a "garbage in, garbage out" mentality. It may go bankrupt or it may shuffle along for a few years before being acquired by someone else—but either way, it will not survive and thrive as long as its people wander aimlessly through their days. A people without vision will perish.

I witness this aimless wandering when entrepreneurs are not properly motivated at the beginning. I believe everyone is an entrepreneur at heart, but too many entrepreneurs get started for the wrong reason. They get started because they're running away from something instead of running toward something. They're tired of having to take orders, so they romanticize the idea of being their own boss. They're tired of not making enough money, so they come up with a get-rich-quick concept. They're tired of going into the office, driving in rush hour traffic, so they want to work from home.

In contrast, successful entrepreneurs have a picture of what they're working toward; they have the end in mind, and it's something that incites a passion within them. Yes, we should learn from the challenges of past jobs, but those challenges shouldn't be the driving inspiration for our future. A car, for instance, has a large windshield and a comparably small rearview mirror. When we drive, our primary focus is moving forward. Occasionally, we might look to learn what's behind us, but that information doesn't determine our destination.

If we're not happy in our current job, we should study ourselves and make sure we know why. Often people experience unhappiness when they operate outside of their gifts; when they drive outside of their lane. When you're not in your traffic lane, something bad usually happens; you might get in an accident or get a ticket. When you're not in your job lane, the consequences come in the form of a lack of achievement and a lack of productivity. They come in the form of fear, doubt, and worry.

People working outside their lanes survive by performing at the minimum necessary level. But entrepreneurs operating outside their lanes cannot survive. That's why the best visions are summoned from our core gifts. For me, I knew that I thrived when serving others, and I thrived within the food business. I operated within my gifts when I developed a vision of an outstanding restaurant. On the other hand, if I had tried to develop a plan for a home-based accounting business, I would've surely failed. I needed to be in a restaurant and constantly interacting with people.

The book of Proverbs says, "A man's gift makes room for him, and brings him before great men."[3] When you're operating within your gift, within your swag, you're operating within your place of strength. This makes room for your success and brings you before the people who can contribute to your success.

---

3. Proverbs 18:16.

The Plan Follows the Vision

A business plan is important, but the vision comes before the plan. If you've read my first book, *A Leap of Faith*, you might recall my good friend Archie Tolar. He was a college friend and also a colleague of mine. After I left Chicago, Archie went to work for Bil-Mar Foods. He was in charge of a line of deli meats, and part of his job was to go out to restaurants and do cuttings (on-site taste, texture, and quality comparisons with other deli products). Archie was an entrepreneur at heart. He wanted to start his own business, but he didn't really have a vision. He decided to open his own deli restaurant.

Archie is one of the hardest workers I know, and he went to work on his plan. He developed a detailed business plan and secured financing through an SBA loan. He found a storefront in a strip mall, moved in, and developed his menu. He did a great job, and I was very proud of him. But he hadn't thought through his long-term vision before implementing his plan. There was nothing special about what he was offering. The strip mall was mostly empty and didn't provide enough traffic. Although he was adequately capitalized and the bank had been impressed with his plan, the deli failed.

After that, I hired him to be a consultant to my stores in Michigan. He would drive from Chicago and work for me ten days out of the month. I put his creative spirit to work. He would listen to my vision on various projects, and then implement them.

But after a while, the traveling got to be too much

Staying Out of the Ditch

of a strain on Archie and his family, and he needed to stay in Chicago. I gave him a reference to McDonald's in that area, and he landed a job. They put him in an entry-level position, however, and gave him little hope of advancing anytime soon. In that job, he was frustrated and unproductive. His entrepreneurial spirit hadn't died, but it wasn't getting used. He wasn't using his gifts.

Archie yearned again to open his own restaurant. But this time, fresh from his experience with implementing my visions, he made an effort to imagine exactly what he wanted to do. Over time, an image unfolded. He wanted to open a soul food restaurant with upscale service in the inner city of Chicago. He could see it. It was unique. He could see the menu. It would be anchored around chicken and waffles. He could see what type of location he wanted. He could see the employees' uniforms. He could see the layout. He saw the name: Blue Soul. I flew down to coach him, and I could see he was totally on fire for this idea. You could see it in his eyes.

Archie followed his vision. He waited until the right location became available, and three years ago, he opened Blue Soul. He had struggles, of course. Almost all restaurants do when they first get started. But he survived, and recently, he opened a second location. He's going strong.

In his first attempt, Archie led with the business plan. In the second, he led with the vision. And that made all the difference.

Paint a Target

Business plans are useful because we take the details of our business and write them down. Recording them helps us remember them and holds us more accountable to their objectives. In the same way, recording your vision is also important. Something special happens when thoughts are made into words and words are put on paper. They move from the spirit world to the flesh. They become faith applied to action. A vision is harder to ignore when it's written down, especially when it's written and posted in prominent places. It serves as a constant reminder, just like the signs did in my restaurants.

Another way you can "record" your vision is to share it with people you trust. Good friends and family can hold you accountable to your plans. You tell them, "I'm going to do this," and they follow up with you periodically to see how you're doing. There's one important caveat about doing this, however. It's important that you tell the right people, since the wrong people (which may in fact be loving members of your family or circle of friends) might put a damper on your dreams for the wrong reasons (such as jealousy or wanting to shield you from risk). The right people will remember your dream; they'll remind you of it. When they think you're on the right track, they'll encourage you onward. When they think you're on the wrong track, they'll nudge you back toward the proper direction.

Leadership expert and author John Maxwell said: "Vision leads the leader. It paints the target. It sparks and fuels the fire within.... Show me a leader without vision, and I'll show you someone who isn't going anywhere."[4] I wrote my vision in prominent places and shared it with people in and out of the industry. It was a target that formed my actions.

> **Freedom Thought**
>
> *How do you want your business to be known to your customers and employees? Take a moment and write down a vision statement for your business. You can change it as your vision grows, but it's important to get something on paper.*
>
> *When you're ready to share it, show it to a few people whose opinions you value. Then, as your business begins and grows, post the statement in prominent places and share it openly and frequently with your employees.*
>
> *The vision will keep you on the right track as you make important decisions along your road of success.*

Through my years of ownership, I continued to carry that vision in my mind every day. When I drove onto the lot in the morning, I looked at the building and premises from a customer's viewpoint. Was there trash on the lot? Was the storefront clean and welcoming? I kept those customer eyes on everything as I walked inside. How did the crew look? Were the customer lines long or short? Did people seem happy? Everything came back to quality, service, and cleanliness. This vision was so important to me, I even had the letters QSC put on my license plate.

When you go into many fast-food restaurants today,

---

4. John Maxwell, *The Maxwell Daily Reader: 365 Days of Insight to Develop the Leader Within You and Influence Those Around You* (Nashville: Thomas Nelson, 2008).

they are deficient in those three areas. Why are the French fries cold? Why do wait times take too long? Why is the floor sticky with used straw wrappers stuck to it? Those areas are deficient because the leadership is deficient. Such owners are in it just for the money; it's just a business to them. It doesn't have any life.

When times got tight and I would have to make a tough decision about a policy or a procedure, I would resort to the vision. Could I make a certain change and still maintain my vision of delivering the service level of an outstanding restaurant operation? Could I still maintain a quality product? Could I maintain an outstanding level of cleanliness? The vision was a constant reminder of where we were going. It was like an antenna on a TV that I could use to calibrate my actions to make sure I was keeping a clear picture.

An owner can feel alone at times. You're charged with leading all your employees, but no one is there to lead you. The big decisions all fall on your shoulders. Fortunately, vision acts as a leader for the entrepreneur.

It's a source of comfort and freedom. It gives you the peace of mind and the courage to make decisions.

It gives you success.

SEVEN
Everything in Its Season

When I was a boy, I wanted to play basketball and go to the NBA. I tried out for my high school basketball team twice. I hustled and demonstrated a competitive drive that many of my teammates didn't have. But I didn't make the cut either time. I was short and not naturally fast.

I never stopped dreaming, however. Dreaming about my future was a hobby of mine. Today, there are more than four hundred players in the NBA—most of them African American. But there are 318 African American McDonald's owners. The odds are easier to get into the NBA than to become a McDonald's owner. So the way I look at it, I made it to the NBA! I tapped into my Natural Born Abilities (my NBA) to achieve my dream.

Entrepreneurship is a journey; therefore, our vision must go on a journey too. You may develop a picture of a new business, and then as you develop experience in that area, your vision will grow and change. That is natural and good. My vision today of improving the lives of 4 million people has changed dramatically from my days of envisioning Ken's Hot Dog Stands. Allowing your vision the flexibility to change will make it stronger. It may become bigger than you ever imagined.

We are made to be entrepreneurs, but we are not made to start or buy a business and camp there the rest of our lives. Entrepreneurship is about more than being one's own boss. It's about movement and growth. Once we start a business, we must continue to develop and refine our vision. We will face obstacles, and our vision will be essential to overcoming those obstacles. And if we're a true entrepreneur, the time will come to sell the business and move on to the next adventure. Our vision will guide us in the proper timing and direction for that move.

Ripening Fruit

Every living thing has a life cycle: birth, toddlerhood, then childhood, followed by adolescence, young adulthood, mature adulthood, aging adulthood, and death. In my way of thinking, a business venture is also a living thing. It has a life cycle. You give birth to your vision, then it grows through infancy and develops until it is walking. You can see it clearly; it is moving forward. Then as your vision goes through the teenage years, you make your preparations—get your experience and draw up plans. Later, the dream is ready to leave home and live on its own. It's time to open the doors to

Everything in Its Season

a full-fledged adult. The business then peaks, and later, ultimately, it will decline in some way. Sales will level off as the novelty and competition grow. Or your passion fades as your creative energy burns to move toward the next challenge.

Life has its seasons, and so does entrepreneurship. It's important to know what season you're in when following your vision. If we pick an apple off a tree too early, it's going to be unripened—too hard. If we implement our vision too early—before we're ready, or before the right location or deal becomes available—success will come too hard. Likewise, if we pick the apple too late, it will be rotten. If we wait too long to follow our dream, the opportunity will pass, and we won't be able to partake of it.

Timing is everything. In Paul's letter to the Galatians, he says, "And let us not grow weary while doing good, for in due season we shall reap if we do not lose heart."[1] At the proper time, in the proper season, we will reap the harvest if we continue in doing good. Clearly, by "doing good," Paul meant we should act with generosity, integrity, and a spirit of service toward others. But I believe we also do good by following God's call for our lives and living a life according to that purpose.

So how do we figure out what season we're in? How do we perfect the timing of our vision and not act prematurely or too late? The only answer takes us back to faith. We need to spend time with God—time praying and

---
1. Galatians 6:9.

reading—and in quiet and thoughtful meditation. That gives you the peace and distance you need to determine if you're ready (if you've learned enough, networked with the right people, found the right location, etc.), or if you're unnecessarily postponing your dream because you're afraid.

The opening verses in the book of Psalms tell us, "Blessed is the man who walks not in the counsel of the ungodly . . . but his delight is in the law of the LORD, and in His law he meditates day and night. He shall be like a tree planted by the rivers of water, that brings forth its fruit in its season, whose leaf also shall not wither; and whatever he does shall prosper."[2] If we meditate on the Lord, we will prosper in our season.

A few years ago, I spoke to a group of businesspeople from a financial services company in Detroit. I gave a presentation on staying motivated during tough and trying times. The financial services market in Detroit had experienced significant decline for quite some time. I told them that life is about change and choices—their business was changing, and they would either need to create new visions to stay successful, or they would need to develop an exit strategy to get out and start something new.

Afterward, Clarence spoke with me and said he wanted to branch out and start his own tax preparation business. Clarence had worked for the same firm for many years, and he had developed an excellent reputation for customer service. He was confident he could use his knowl-

---
2. Psalm 1:1–3.

edge and reputation to become successful on his own.

Clarence ended up becoming a coaching client of mine, and I walked him through the principles for becoming a successful entrepreneur. Eventually, he met with one of the leading tax preparation companies about opening a franchise, but they could not offer him a deal that he thought was fair.

Clarence had faith enough in his vision not to take a bad deal. Unfortunately, I've often seen people jump on the bad deal because they're too eager or they think another deal won't come along. They don't understand the concept of the right season. I saw this at McDonald's where potential owners would get "arches in their eyes." McDonald's would offer them a highly enticing store, but the overall deal would not be in the owner's favor. They would take it anyway, and this decision often led to pain down the road.

Clarence was heartbroken when he turned the company down. He kept pursuing his dream, however, and he kept networking with people and trying to learn about potential opportunities.

During that time his mother became ill, and his father had difficulty taking care of her. Clarence decided to go ahead and resign his position with the financial services company. He had seen too many colleagues get laid off, and he felt it was only a matter of time before the same thing happened to him. His parents needed him, and since he had saved his money, he could afford to stay home and honor his parents with his time and attention.

I lost track of Clarence for a while, but eventually, I received a phone call from him. He had enjoyed many blessings from spending time with his parents and from being a caregiver. It was a time that enriched his life, and he was grateful for the opportunity. He also wanted to let me know he had received a phone call from a different financial firm that was interested in having him start an agency. They were aware of his reputation and had contacted him, unsolicited, to see if he was interested.

For Clarence, he had to wait until the season was right. If he had jumped at the first opportunity, he would've taken a bad deal, and he would've been unavailable for his parents. When the season was right, the opportunity ripened, and he took advantage of it.

Deal or No Deal

In addition to practicing your faith, you can test whether you're in the right season by practicing patience and avoiding impulsivity. In terms of personal money management, financial expert Dave Ramsey recommends you wait thirty days before making any major purchases, like a new car or a new TV. This gives you time to get past the impulse and see if you're still excited about spending those dollars. People usually choose not to make the purchase after such a period. In particular, high-pressure sales situations (such as when you're given a very brief period of time to make up your mind) almost always involve purchases you can't risk making. We can apply the same philosophy to making

Everything in Its Season

major entrepreneurial decisions. Give yourself time to make sure the opportunity aligns with your vision and falls into the appropriate season. Take a breath. Talk it over with trusted people. Don't rush into anything.

Faith in your vision means you don't compromise it for the bad deal. I've seen too many people stuck between the bad deal and fear—fear that they'll never get another opportunity. When I'm coaching them, I tell them, "Not having another opportunity might be a fact, but it isn't the truth." Yes, they might not get another opportunity with that company or in that area, but that doesn't mean it's over. There are other companies and other locations. Scared money can't make money, and God is the only one who gets to say when it's over.

Desperation to get out of your current situation might motivate you, but that's despair not vision. We can't despise small beginnings. We need to prosper where we're planted and use our vision to guide us and help us get ready.

Business ownership is like the game of chess; you make moves based on your long-term strategy. In chess, the first moves are often made by the pawns. Those moves might seem insignificant to the uneducated observer, but they play into the long-term strategy. Other moves might even require the sacrifice of a piece. That may seem foolhardy to the uneducated observer, but again, these moves play into the long-term strategy. To start a new business, you may need to start with small, seemingly insignificant moves—you might attend some industry association meetings during your off-hours. You may need to sacrifice the urgency of your dreams—staying and prospering in your current position—so you can build your savings and knowledge and be better prepared. But small moves—as long as they are legitimate moves and migrate you toward your vision—only serve to make your eventual success more probable.

Jazz in the Playland

Developing your vision is an ongoing process. It gets you through the obstacles you will face. Some seasons will give you smooth waters; other seasons will give you rough seas. Most days will present you with areas of your business that need to be improved—areas where vision will lead you to a more successful venture.

In one of my stores, we had a large Playland area for the kids. It seated fifty people and consumed a huge amount of electricity to light and cool the place. During the summertime, I noticed that Playland would go mostly unused on Saturdays. Everyone was at the beach or having a picnic. They didn't come in. So I put my vision to work and tried to come up with an alternative way to use the space. I was already paying for it and paying my staff to be on duty; I needed bodies in the chairs.

I love jazz music, so I eventually came up with an idea to bring in jazz bands. I pictured a quartet in the room every Saturday night. I saw white tablecloths and silver decorations on the walls. I saw a hostess seating people and taking their orders. It was something completely different, but my faith and vision allowed me to see something completely out of the box for a McDonald's restaurant.

Within a week, we implemented our first jazz night. We had everything decorated the way I had pictured. Two people showed up that first Saturday. But it grew, and before long we had filled the room. Many of the people who showed up were first-time customers. They would come up to me and tell me I had the cleanest McDonald's they had ever been in. Many of them returned when they saw the level of quality and service we provided.

Another time, one of my lobbies had to undergo some significant renovations. The lobby was shut down for a month, and we lost all of our walk-in traffic (which constituted 30 percent of our sales). I still had the same number of employees on my payroll; I didn't want to let people go, especially for what was a temporary problem. Again, I put my problem-solving, visionary skills to work. I figured if people won't come to us, then we'll go to them. I came up with the idea of

> **Freedom Thought**
>
> *Life will bring you many changes just as it has up to this point. As an entrepreneur, you must commit yourself to continual growth. Not just growth of your business but of yourself and your vision.*
>
> *Everything has its season. Be ready to pounce when the right opportunity comes along, but wary of the bad deal. Then as your business grows, be prepared for the day when it's time to move on.*
>
> *Entrepreneurship is about movement. It's a journey, not a destination.*

delivering to nearby businesses: we called it McDonald's Mobile. Businesses would fax in their order, and my staff (now better utilized) would drive the filled order out to them. It was another solution you didn't find too often at other McDonald's restaurants.

Those solutions show the benefits of a well-developed vision. When things are not going right, you go left. You turn roadblocks into opportunities. You sit down, relax, spend time in meditation, and see what images develop.

I traveled through my years under the arches by adhering to my vision. Eventually, however, your vision should bring you to the end of your time in the business, just as it did for me. I believe businesses are made to be sold. You start them, you build them, and then you pass them on to the next person so they can take them to the next level, and so you can start the next great thing. You become a subject matter expert in an opportunity, grow rich in the niche, and then find the next opportunity. You need an exit strategy.

When we look at wildly successful people like Donald Trump, we should ask how many ventures has he started and then later passed on to someone else? Sometimes he sells them, other times he leaves them to be managed by someone else, but he is always looking for the next opportunity. His vision keeps morphing and growing and it begins with the end in mind. How will you get out? When and where? How long will you operate at this level? Will you sell? Will you expand and delegate? Will you franchise? Business owners can't begin that conversation with themselves down the road. The demands of entrepreneurship can be overwhelming if we don't plan our long-term actions from the beginning. Instead of seeing the next steps, we'll feel trapped by the tasks of ownership. That's when people get stuck and camp out.

Success is a journey. It doesn't sit down. It keeps moving. Vision must join us on that journey. Through vision, we can picture the beginning, middle, and end. Through vision, we can have the strength to start over again.

Faith sets us on our voyage, and vision guides us along the way. That's how an entrepreneur lives in freedom every day.

PURPOSE

EIGHT
Answering the Why

As I worked my way through the food industry, I carried two entrepreneurial dreams. The first, I've already mentioned: Ken's Hot Dog Stands. The other was going to be a consulting business called Food Services Solutions. My friend Archie and I spent many hours thinking about that business.

I considered every job I took to be temporary. I called them *paid internships*. They were opportunities for me to learn new skills and to provide services—to make a difference for the company that employed me. I never considered those jobs as opportunities to camp out—collecting a paycheck and making a minimal impact. I wanted to learn what I could, blow people away with the impact of my efforts, and then move on to the next "internship."

Over time, I worked for companies on both the supplier side and the restaurant side of the food industry, including fast-food restaurants and high-end restaurants. I understood the food business. I also understood the systems that those companies utilized. The word *system* can stand for Save YourSelf Time, Energy, and Money, and I had learned a system for how to run a food operation efficiently—doing more with less—while improving customer service.

Archie and I believed we could take our knowledge of systems and make an impact in the industry. So many restaurants struggle and sometimes fail because they're poorly run. Time is wasted. Food is wasted. Because their systems are ineffective or nonexistent, employee morale and performance suffers and customer satisfaction declines. Ultimately a restaurant cannot stay in business in a situation like that. There's too much competition. But Archie and I could make a difference; I knew we could. We could take the experience we had garnered from companies like Quaker, Wendy's, Tyson, Nabisco, AWG, and Kraft, and help entrepreneurs implement and execute the systems—such as training systems and ordering systems—that would make them a success.

Life brought me new opportunities, however, and I never started Food Service Solutions. Yet things didn't turn out much differently than I had hoped. In my first book, I told the story of how I got discovered by McDonald's. I had gone to a McDonald's open house to sell them on the Food Service Solutions concept. At that time, the McDonald's brand was not doing well. The company suffered under a general perception that their stores were slow, dirty, and unfriendly. I thought I could make a difference in some of their stores as a consultant. I could show them how to improve their overall customer experience.

At the open house, I caught their attention. But instead of contracting me as a consultant, they ended up hiring me and eventually putting me on a track to acquire my own stores. My vision changed, but my purpose never did. My purpose was to make a difference—to make an impact in the experiences and lives of the people who worked for me and bought my food. I brought that purpose from my Food Services Solutions dream and applied it to running a McDonald's business.

Significance

God has a plan for your life. You have a destiny and a purpose. It's been said that we have two birthdays: the day we are born into this world and the day we figure out why we were born. The plan is already set for us, and it's our job to stay close enough to God to figure it out. He created the universe and gave it order, and you are part of that order. He put you here for a specific time and purpose. Psalm 37 says: "The steps of a good man are ordered by the LORD."[1] When we spend time with him and seek his guidance, he directs our steps toward our purpose.

Since your purpose is planned by God, the world inevitably benefits when you follow it. You are a piece in the puzzle of God's plan, and you need to place yourself

---

1. Psalm 37:23.

within the puzzle to make it complete. In his book *Halftime: Moving from Success to Significance*, Bob Buford tells us that we can divide our lives into two halves, with the midpoint usually falling between the ages of thirty and fifty.

During the first part of our lives, we are focused on learning, earning money, and getting ahead. From my perspective, this is when we're preparing for our entrepreneurial life. We're taking advantage of school and relevant jobs (paid internships), and we're accumulating the wealth we need to invest in a successful future business.

In the second half of our lives, according to Buford, we need to shift to a life of significance. That's when we take on more risks and live beyond the immediate. By making that shift, we'll experience a life of purpose and see the fulfillment of our life's mission. If we don't make that shift to significance, then we end up joining the ranks of those who are coasting their way into retirement. Those who, at the end of their lives, will look back and wonder what it was all for. Those who do make the shift will look back on their lives and see a work of art. "The great and glorious masterpiece of man is how to live with a purpose," said philosopher Michel de Montaigne. Pursuing that masterpiece gives us the freedom to live out our destiny.

My purpose wasn't money. Impact drives income, so I believed if I made an impact, the money would follow.

Answering the Why

When you impact someone's life, when you impact someone's business brand, you're going to make money. I believe my experience has been a testimony to that. Money was the fruit of how I treated my employees. Money was the fruit of how I treated my customers and my community. Money was the fruit of my thoughts, habits, and decisions—all of which were focused on making a difference.

I once knew of a guy who made fantastic chicken wings. I'll call him Darrell. He would hold parties for big sports events like the Final Four and the Super Bowl, and he would make tray after tray of different kinds of wings. People loved them. "You're great at making these," his friends told him. "You should start a business."

Darrell hated his current job, so he was intrigued by his friends' frequent encouragement. He enjoyed cooking, especially for his parties, so he eventually decided to take a leap. He quit his job and opened a chicken wings and pizza store on a heavily traveled road in his town. But he was never able to attract much customer traffic. After seven months, he closed his doors for the last time.

Why did Darrell want to go into business for himself? From what I observed, he went into business because he liked to cook chicken wings and he disliked his job. Was there a need for a wings restaurant in his area? Did people want one? Did he provide a superior product and service? Could he make an impact and distinguish himself? Did he have a plan to make an impact with employees and customers and turn that goodwill into a prospering business? Those questions didn't seem to be significant to him. He didn't have a legitimate answer to the question: *Why?* His business didn't have a purpose—other than to get him out of a job he wasn't excited about.

God has a plan and a unique purpose for everyone. It's our job to follow him, spend time with him, and discern what that purpose is. It is not our job to avoid the discerning of our purpose in order to get out of a bad job situation. That rarely works well.

If I just want money, then I should play the stock market. If I just want to do something fun, then I should develop a hobby. When we're considering starting a business, we have to ask ourselves: Why? What's my purpose? Why do I want a business? Why do I want success? The finer details of these answers will be different for everyone. But for entrepreneurs, our overall purpose should be the same. My purpose at McDonald's was *to make a difference*. To make a difference in the experiences and needs of my customers, in the lives of my employees, and in the welfare of my community.

As with faith and vision, purpose allows us to stay focused. Friedrich Nietzsche said, "He who has a *why* can endure any *how*." You can figure out how to do it, if you have a reason for doing it. If there isn't a need to be filled, then a business will struggle. But if you find a need, you can figure out the *how* of responding to that need.

Organizations are divided into for-profit and nonprofit entities. We look at nonprofit companies as having a service mission. Their purpose is to help other people advance their lives in some way. But we have a misconception that for-profit companies exist to advance the lives of the owners and no one else—that they are self-centered organizations, that they have no service component to their purpose. I reject that idea. We are all born to service. It's been said that "Service is the price we pay for taking up the space we occupy."

External and Internal Customers

In the history of the world, no business owner has ever operated on his or her own. To do that, you would have to be your only employee and your only customer. Business ownership is about serving people and their needs.

I got into McDonald's through service. As I mentioned, I was working on weekends as a waiter at a high-end restaurant called Lorenzo's. Although it was a moonlighting job, I put everything into it. I tried to give my customers an exceptional experience—an experience they wouldn't forget. I took care of those people as if they were my family. The service I provided was so phenomenal, customers kept coming back and requesting my tables. I stood out among the other servers at the restaurant and among restaurant servers in general. I was noticed.

I was noticed, in particular, by Edie Waddell, an executive with McDonald's. As a customer at Lorenzo's, she was so impressed by my level of service, that when I ran into her at that McDonald's open house, she couldn't recruit me fast enough. That job at Lorenzo's wasn't about me. It wasn't about collecting an extra paycheck so I could buy some nice things for myself. It was about servanthood. When exceptional service gets noticed, what happens? People come back. People want to work with you. People will even pay more for what you have to offer (as my high tips proved). Then money will follow.

When I opened my own business, not only did I continue my exceptional customer service philosophy but I expanded it. As an owner, I had two sets of customers to serve—external customers and internal customers, also known as employees.

During my employee career, I was blessed to work for some excellent companies and bosses who had a servant mentality. But I also worked for people who didn't value me. I was a cost item to them, a number, an afterthought. I witnessed firsthand what that approach did to morale. I witnessed what lower morale did to customer satisfaction—employees weren't motivated to serve their customers. And I witnessed how low customer satisfaction negatively impacted the financial performance.

As I formulated my vision for my future restaurants,

I was determined to deliver outstanding satisfaction to my internal customers as well. Your internal customers are the ones closest to you. They're the ones who hear what you have to say. More important, they're the ones who watch your actions. If you're not serving them, then they're not going to serve you.

No doubt, customer service is on the decline. We see the evidence of that every day. But it's not because employees are naturally inconsiderate, lazy, or shiftless. It's because they're all like Mick Jagger, singing, "I can't get no satisfaction." While they're supposed to serve the customers, no one is serving them. There is no joy in their jobs.

Purpose through Understanding

In my restaurants, we had a concept called "management on a personal basis." By design, my managers and I got to know each employee. We got to know their families and personal interests. We also got to know their strengths and what opportunities they wanted to pursue. Then we developed a plan to put them in position to flourish and tap their fullest potential. We also went to significant lengths to make them feel valued, including letting them eat the restaurant's food for free, giving them gift certificates on their birthdays, and giving away televisions and stereos at employee rallies. One of the most important things I did was to pay my employees more than other stores. I started people at far above the minimum wage. Other stores would offer minimum wage, but that didn't inspire any loyalty. Those employees would always be on the lookout for something better. I wanted my employees to be satisfied with their pay and want to earn it by satisfying their customers.

Whenever financial times get tight, companies start claiming the need to reduce and control labor. Labor is a cost item to them that must be managed. Labor is an "unfortunate part" of doing business. They say reducing labor is *addition by subtraction*—they'll subtract people and increase profits. But my mind-set never was to reduce and control labor. I wanted to increase traffic and sales. My plan was to make sure we had enough people to provide excellent service, and then to watch our traffic skyrocket. I called it *multiplication through addition*.

Through focusing on my internal customers, I was able to develop strategic partners; I was able to go from just having employees to having a high performance team. In order to give satisfaction to my external customers, I knew I had to make my internal customers happy.

As entrepreneurs, we need to understand our employees and be familiar with their unique situations. We have to work with them and not treat them like some enemy force that wants to take advantage of us. That isn't always easy, but it needs to be done.

For example, let's say an owner has an employee

who's supposed to work today, but she calls and says she can't make it. Her child's sitter has canceled on her, and she can't leave her children.

The owner offers little sympathy. "You're on the schedule," he says. "You've got to get to work. It's your responsibility."

However, it's not completely her responsibility. It is the owner's responsibility to figure out his workforce and allow for the unexpected. She has a situation for which she might not have a solution. She won't get paid for not coming to work; she's already losing out. The owner needs to work with her.

If he threatens her with, "Come to work or you'll lose your job," what might happen? Maybe she'll scramble and find a way, but what frame of mind will she be in? How will she treat the customers? How will the owner be able to remind her that 100 percent customer satisfaction is the goal? Yes, she's an employee with a job to do and minimum expectations for performing that job. But she's also a person with needs and challenges.

> **Freedom Thought**
>
> What is your why? Why do you want to be in business for yourself? Being your own boss or making lots of money are motivators, but not answers to the question of why. An entrepreneur's purpose should be to live a life of significance.
>
> We need to make an impact in the experiences of our customers and employees. Money is the fruit of living in our purpose. Impact will drive income. Before moving forward, you need to answer two questions: What has God called you to do? How will you make a positive difference through your business?

As entrepreneurs, part of our purpose is to meet our employees where they are and serve them.

In the next two chapters, I will discuss the freedom of living in true purpose—the purpose of making a difference with the people with whom you interact the most through your business—your customers and employees. That is the destiny of significance that God desires for our lives. That is a freedom principle that creates *true* entrepreneurial success.

NINE
People before Profits

In 2006 ABC News[1] profiled Costco and its cofounder and CEO, Jim Sinegal. At the time of the profile, 45 million shoppers visited Costco, which was the nation's fourth-largest retailer, earning sales of more than $52 billion. How did Costco achieve such success? According to Sinegal, they provided a good financial return to their shareholders by adhering to their code of ethics: they obeyed the law, they took care of the customers, and they took care of their people.

Costco has developed a strong, loyal workforce. In 2006 they paid an average wage of $17 per hour, 40 percent more than Costco's main club warehouse rival, Sam's Club. They had the lowest turnover rate in the retail industry, five times lower than Wal-Mart. They offered health care coverage to more than 90 percent of their workers.

At times, Costco has gotten flack from Wall Street analysts who believe the company could

1. Adam B. Goldberg and Bill Ritter, "Costco CEO Finds Pro-Worker Means Profitability," ABC News, 20/20, August 2, 2006, http://abcnews.go.com/2020/Business/story?id=1362779.

make even more money if they cut back on labor expenses. But Sinegal counters, "Wall Street is in the business of making money between now and next Tuesday. We're in the business of building an organization, an institution that we hope will be here 50 years from now."[2] That sounds a lot like *purpose*. Through treating his people well, Sinegal is building an institution. Through his business practices, he wants to make a difference.

Sinegal travels constantly on the corporate jet, visiting up to twelve stores a day. He wears a name tag with just his first name on it, like everyone else. According to the authors of the article, he could be mistaken for a stock clerk due to his regular appearance. He believes Costco should be a company that's on a first-name basis with everyone.

Costco doesn't have an advertising budget. Instead, it relies on its employees. "Imagine that you have 120,000 loyal ambassadors out there who are constantly saying good things about Costco," says Sinegal.[3] Those aren't employees; those are strategic partners. They are an integral piece to the amazing success of the company.

The Most Important Asset

To live within your entrepreneurial purpose, I believe you can never put profit before people. Treating labor as an arbitrary cost item to be slashed may give you a bump

---

2. Ibid.
3. Ibid.

in profits, like the Wall Street analysts believed would happen with Costco, but that bump is only temporary. In order for me to have sustainable, long-term growth, I needed to invest in my people.

The accounting practices in the business world are messed up. When we invest in equipment or facilities, it's called an asset. It has value. But putting money into your employees is called an expense. It's "blowing money" on labor. But how can you blow money on human potential? How can it be a waste to invest in the most precious asset in the world—a human being? At Brown Food Group, we always rejected that way of thinking.

If you're not investing in people, if you're not involving and engaging them in a strategic way, how are you going to manage a complex and sensitive system like a business? Take a look at businesses that failed in the last few years. What were their people policies? What was their workforce morale like? How did they interact with their customers? In many cases, I bet they had a deficient people policy. They put profits before people. Sometimes there are other external factors, like being located in the wrong place, or customer trends that are misread or shift abruptly in a new direction. But often, when a failed business owner says, "No one came to my store," it actually means, "No one wanted to come to my business because my employees didn't make them want to come." People problems invariably show up in other areas—low customer volume, low dollars per transaction, low repeat business, slow service, a poor quality product—but the true source of the problems comes down to one central issue—the owner forgot his or her purpose.

As an entrepreneur, I considered the mission of developing people to be central to my purpose. A few weeks before I wrote this, I heard about reality star Heidi Montag and how she had ten plastic surgery operations in one day. She had told *People* magazine she was "obsessed" with plastic surgery, and she just wanted to be "the best me"[4] she could be. She got a lot of publicity for her decision, but I think most people who heard about it felt pity for her. She didn't realize that being "the best me" was an inside job. She didn't feel good on the inside, and no amount of cosmetic improvements could change that for her.

Life is an inside job for everyone, and I believed my purpose as a leader was to help people tap into their fullest potential. Ultimately people will forget most of what you say, and even most of what you do, but they will never, ever forget how you made them feel. People don't care what you know until they know how much you care.

Whenever I hired someone, I tried to get to know them—get to know their strengths and aspirations. I wanted them to reach their fullest potential within my

---
4. Jennifer Garcia, "Heidi Montag Obsessed with Being 'Perfect.'" *People*, January 25, 2010, 80–88.

company. And if they went as far as they could go within my company, I wanted them to be able to leave and continue to grow and prosper.

Cynthia-driven Income

After I first opened the new restaurant, a woman named Cynthia came to me looking for a job. She was a pleasant woman but looked like things had not always been easy for her. She had grown up on the south side of Chicago. She had tattoos up and down her arms.

Cynthia had applied for a manager's position at another McDonald's, but they would only start her at $7.50 per hour. She was hoping for a similar position with me but with more money. I had to tell her no. One of the main components of my purpose was to develop people, so I didn't hire people directly into the management level. I developed people to become managers. I told Cynthia I would pay her the same amount as the other store, but she would need to start on the night crew and work her way up. Cynthia took the challenge.

She humbled herself. She was focused. We trained her on the position, and she became proficient at it. But she butted heads with another worker on that shift. Her name was Koran. She was very good at her job, a wonderful employee, but Cynthia tried to tell her what to do. They both took a lot of pride in the performance of the shift, but they didn't always see eye to eye.

It was obvious that Cynthia didn't have a lot of skills, and she didn't look the part of a successful career person. I could've held all that against her. I could've tried to "protect" my business from the influence of someone like that. But my purpose was to make a difference, to have an impact. I wanted to make a difference in Cynthia's life as much as she wanted to make a difference on the night shift.

After a few months, Koran and I were talking one evening, and she said, "You know, Mr. Brown, Cynthia is a good leader."

I was surprised, given how the two of them didn't always seem to get along. "How so?" I asked.

"She's tough on the outside. She expects you to work hard. But she wants what's best for the restaurant. She leads by example."

I had seen that commitment to excellence in Cynthia too, but Koran's comments really brought it home. Cynthia commanded respect by the way she approached her life and her job. She was no-nonsense and focused on her purpose. I took a chance, and when an opening came up, I promoted her to night manager.

She struggled with some parts of the job. She did not have great computer skills and did not pick up those skills quickly. However, we accentuated the positive, and I brought in my sister, Regina, to help her with the things that challenged Cynthia. In addition to her continued leadership abilities, another positive was her willingness to learn. I didn't judge Cynthia's skill level; I only judged her heart, and soon found she had what it took to be a success. Over time she made it happen. She became a fantastic night manager.

Then I lost our store manager when he moved on to bigger things, and I promoted Cynthia to that position. Cynthia, of the tattoos and troubled past, was now running my store. Again she struggled somewhat to learn the new skills. "I'm not very good at this," she said one day.

"You don't need to be good at this yet. You just keep doing what you do, and I'll put the people around you to help you succeed."

Again I brought in Regina and a few consultants from McDonald's to assist Cynthia with developing her skills. I invested in her. I challenged her and pushed her, but I tried my best to make her comfortable. Before long, she mastered the job. She led by example, and she made others around her want to be better by the example she set. She made a difference in the pride they took in their jobs. And she provided unrelenting customer service.

I invested in Cynthia, and the return on my investment was phenomenal. Under her watch, the annual sales for that store increased from $1.3 million to $2.3 million. It was incredible.

I didn't learn the details of Cynthia's background

until my retirement party many years later. She had been in and out of prison three times. She had experienced bouts with alcohol and drugs. She had run from Chicago and come to Michigan following a "rope of hope"—a fervent attempt to get control of her life. At the time she first walked through my doors, she knew only one person in the entire state of Michigan.

Her children had been taken from her. By the grace of God, her parents were able to take custody of the children and keep them within the family. After she worked for me for a while, she was able to buy her own home. Later, she succeeded enough that her oldest daughter was allowed to come to Michigan and live with her. Eventually her daughter started working for me also. Then her other children were allowed to join her, and they were a family again. She felt good about herself, and she became an ambassador for my company. Whenever we needed employees, she would encourage good people to come join the Brown Food Group.

At my retirement party, she thanked me. "You believed in me," she told me. "You treated me with respect and dignity. You valued my growth, and you stretched me. You changed the way I looked at the world." That was huge for me. Because I had remembered my purpose, I had made a difference in her life. I had done nothing extraordinary; I had simply believed in her. When she struggled, I supported her. When she needed to grow, I invested in her. The end result proved my belief in putting people first. Her spirits soared, and so did my profits. Impact drove income.

Not Just Any Ordinary Leader

My purpose was to give people more than a job. I wanted to give them life skills and self-worth. As a McDonald's owner, I knew many of my employees received their first paycheck ever from me. I had one employee who had worked for many years as a barber, but had never experienced steady pay until he worked for me. He was a grown man, not a young student, and when I handed him his first paycheck, he cried. He was so thankful.

That's why I paid my employees, including my newest hires, well above minimum wage. Although I caught flack for that from other owners, I wanted my people to feel valued and to care about my company. If Cynthia had taken the first job offer at the other restaurant, do you think she would have felt valued like she did at my store? Would that job have made an impact in her life and the life of her family? Would that restaurant have seen such an increase in sales? I don't know the answer to those questions, but the odds are the answer is no. She felt valued and cared for at my business.

Every entrepreneur will say they want to provide 100 percent customer satisfaction, and they want 100 percent effort from their people. But if we pay them just enough to get by, how are we going to meet either of those goals? That's why I paid my people more. If I wanted my sales to grow, if I wanted to grow my vision, if I wanted to reap the harvest, I had to plant seeds. But I planted seeds by using more than just money. I wanted to know my employees personally, and I wanted them to feel comfortable around me. When I walked into my restaurants each day, I greeted my employees with a hug and a friendly handshake. Many of them came from Senegal, Africa, and I would ask them, "How's your family?" They were working for me and sending money back home to their families, and I couldn't imagine how hard that must have been for them.

I mentioned earlier that I put our vision statement at the front of our employee handbook. Just below the statement I wrote, "People are our most important asset. People will be valued at every level of our organization." I didn't put those words at the front of an investor handbook—a handbook for strangers to look at. I put it at the front of the handbook for the very people who would hold me accountable to those words. I wanted my employees to know where I stood, and I wanted the prominence of that principle to hold me accountable.

As business owners, I think our purpose is not just to be a leader—to lead our people in the day-to-day activities of our business—but to be a *strategic* leader. Strategic leaders put demands on their people's potential, create new opportunities for them to succeed, and help them realize their potential.

When I begin a coaching project with business leaders, in addition to asking to see their vision statement, I spend the first day trailing them. I watch their habits. I sit in on meetings and observe how they interact with others. Are their employees treated with value? Who is serving whom? Is the owner living up to the vision he or she set forth? Everyone can talk a good game about valuing employees. But often, when owners come to me because their businesses are struggling, I find there's a disconnect between the talk and the walk.

Flipping the Script

In my business, we flipped the script; we flipped the org chart. In most companies, the owner or CEO sits at the top of the organizational chart (the diagram of boxes that pictures who reports to whom within an organization or department). Then you have a line of vice presidents under him or her, and then a line of high-level managers under them. At the bottom of the chart, you'll find the line workers—the entry-level workers. Most often, those employees are the ones with the most interface with the customers. But those org charts tell me the wrong thing. They tell me that the line workers are the least important, and it's their job to serve the people who sit above them. Ultimately, in such organizations, the chart shows that it's everyone's responsibility to serve the owner or the CEO. But what about the customers? Whose job is it to serve them?

The people who interact with the customers the most are the ones who, day in and day out, add the most value to the business. After establishing the vision and making sure we adhered to that image of success, I recognized that I had the least impact on the daily operations. That honor went to my line workers. The last thing I wanted was for our employees to be focusing their energies on me and not the customer.

A business owner must put their customers first—everybody in their company must be focused on that. There's an old song that says, "I've got my mind on my money, and my money on my mind." You do not want that in your business. You don't want your people worrying about the money. You want them worrying about the customers and the vision. Yes, the money needs to be managed, and managed well, but it can't be the number-one priority.

When I designed our org chart, I turned it upside down. I put the customers at the top. The job of everyone in my restaurants was to serve them. Then came the line workers, then under them came the managers. At the bottom was the owner, Ken Brown. I saw myself as a servant leader. Following my example, my managers saw themselves as servants to the people who reported to them.

Because of our people policies, we didn't experience employee turnover like most fast-food restaurants. When people joined our company, they usually stayed for a long time, until a better opportunity came their way, and then we sent them on with our best wishes. Occasionally someone wouldn't latch on to my vision, and I had to let them go. Even then, however, I would try to take care of them. I would offer them severance or help with getting unemployment insurance, although that drove up my insurance rates. But my business was my dream, my baby, and like we do when we seek childcare for our actual children, I had to be careful about who was caring for my baby. I didn't just want people to work in my business; I wanted them to care about it. I wanted them to care about it the way Cynthia cared about it. If they didn't, I still needed to care for them and make sure they departed in the right way.

Even then, I didn't see those employees in strict categories of bad and good. Employees did make mistakes, sometimes bad ones, and there were consequences. But I also believed in second chances.

At one store, a brother and sister worked for me, and

> **Freedom Thought**
>
> *Will your business need to rely on other people—employees or contractors—to fulfill your vision? How will you make them your most important asset? You can start by developing a flipped org chart, so they know your purpose is to serve them and their purpose is to serve the customers.*
>
> *Then you need to develop a plan that adheres to that chart. Compensation, benefits, perks, training, empowerment, and management attitude can factor into the plan. Many businesses fail because of poor people policies. The more employees feel valued, the more they'll work for your success.*

they had a younger brother who was anxious to join my team. He would come in with his siblings to pick up their paychecks, and he witnessed how well they were treated. When he turned fourteen, I didn't hesitate to hire him.

He was a hard worker just like his brother and sister. He was hungry to learn and focused on the customer. I used to call him a baller—he came ready for the game. Even at fourteen, he had a positive influence on the people around him, and I wasn't the only one who heaped praise upon him. People were attracted to his energy.

But he was young and still maturing, and he got too comfortable. He started reading his own press. Real ballers don't listen to ESPN; they don't read the headlines. They go out every day and stay hungry and work their game. At one point, the young man made a big mistake and broke a major policy. I had no choice. I had to fire him. He knew he had messed up, and he didn't try to argue with me.

A few years later, he came back and asked for his old job back. I believed in second chances, so I stayed in my purpose and rehired him.

He was phenomenal. He had learned his lesson and performed even better than before. My customers loved him.

At my retirement party, he came up to me. Before

I could offer him my hand, he grabbed me and hugged me tighter than anyone. He whispered in my ear, "Mr. Brown, I love you. You helped me become a man."

"What?" I said. I couldn't believe what he had said.

He kept hugging me, right in front of his friends. "You're a role model for me. I'm never going to forget you."

That's purpose. That's making a difference. Employees like that young man, and like Cynthia, made me a success. I had the pleasure of helping them be successful too.

TEN
The Custom of Success

Not all entrepreneurs have employees. But all of us do have other people who support our business. We have suppliers and service providers, and individuals in those companies often support our dreams in crucial ways. They are similar to employees, and we need to make a difference in their lives. We need to lift them up and encourage them. Most of us also have family that supports us—spouses, children, parents, aunts, uncles, cousins. They can affect our success more than anyone. As a family member, it's definitely our purpose to make a difference in their lives. Plus, the better our family life is, the better we will operate within our gifts and the more successful we will be.

Regardless of whether we have employees, suppliers, or family members, however, the one thing all entrepreneurs have are customers—customers and a community of people who live and work around the location of their business. When you make a difference in a customer's day, and when you make an impact in your community, people want to come back to you. You don't have to beg them for sales. You don't have to spend gobs of money on advertising. They *want* to do business with you and they will seek you out.

Remembering the *Why*

Not everything went right when I was a McDonald's owner. Sometimes even my philosophy about purpose and putting people first worked against me. On two separate occasions, I was sued by a former employee. In each case, their level of performance had fallen so far that I was left with no choice; I had to let them go. Still, I treated them generously and gave them long severance packages (something unheard of in the fast-food industry) so they would have time to find another job. I guess they thought my generosity could last forever, so when their severance ran out, they each found an attorney and sued me for more money. And worse, although I believed I wasn't in the wrong, my insurance company wanted to settle in both cases in order to avoid the higher costs of a court battle.

The lawsuits pulled me into a dark valley. I had been standing on the mountain as my sales increased, but now I wondered if I had been wrong all along. Maybe it *was* just about profits. Maybe it was foolish to put people first if some of them were just going to turn around and try to get more out of me. I had been foolish to not get a signed agreement to waive the right to sue in exchange for the severance (a common practice I later learned), but now I wondered if I had been foolish in my entire approach.

Fortunately my valley of doubt didn't last long. I had a group of people who pulled me out of it—my customers.

We had an 800 number on the bags at every McDonald's, and customers could use that number to call the company and offer their feedback. A central McDonald's office would transcribe those calls, and then send them to store owners via e-mail. The calls for many McDonald's would consist mainly of complaints, but almost all of the feedback for my stores came in the form of compliments. The compliments were about the exceptional level of service; the happy, friendly staff; and the spotless, sparkling facilities. One said, "We always go to this McDonald's." Another said, "The people who work there make us feel like royalty!"

I would look at those e-mails and smile. For me, that was what being a business owner was about—making people feel good, having an impact. I would forward the messages to my employees, along with a thank you from me. They were the ones making my customers happy. The high level of customer satisfaction in my stores, and the resulting high sales, would've been impossible without putting my employees ahead of the bottom-line. Yes, I was doing the right thing.

The Custom of Returning

The McDonald's Corporation conducted customer surveys to find out where they needed to improve, and the returning surveys usually highlighted two areas. The second highest problem area was order accuracy: restaurants would mess up the order—they'd forget the fries or stick the wrong sandwich in the bag. But the number-one issue was customer service—specifically, unengaged or rude employees. Employees who acted like the customer was a nuisance bugged people the most. Although that's a common problem (not just in McDonald's but in many businesses), in my experience, it wasn't the employees who should be directly blamed.

When I train executives or business owners, I pay attention to how they talk about their customers. Often it is with a certain disregard. They talk about them in terms of nameless numbers they can manipulate and get something from. Nobody likes to be manipulated, however, and nobody likes to have something taken from them. Customers like to be served. Our goal should be for customers to *want* to return time after time.

The word *customer* comes from the word *custom*, or *habit*, meaning someone who makes it a habit to purchase goods or services from a particular business rather than another similar business in another location. L.L.Bean, which is known for its outstanding customer service, says in its mission statement, "Above all, we wish to avoid having a dissatisfied customer. We consider our customers a part of our organization, and we want them to feel free to make any criticism they see fit in regard to our merchandise or service. Sell practical, tested merchandise at reasonable profit, treat your customers like human beings—and they will always come back."

"They will always come back"—that's a company that knows its purpose!

A typical company in the U.S. loses half of its customers every five years. Given the decline in customer service, it's easy to see why. In addition to not valuing customers, companies are pushing customers further away from contact with its employees. For example, you can see that happening with airlines and banks that force customers to use automated phone systems or Web sites in lieu of actual customer service. People want human contact. They want a smile (whether it's a smile in person or a smile in a voice over the phone). They want a kind word. They want to know they are valued. When a customer has to labor for ten minutes to navigate through an automated phone system, who's doing the work—the company or the customer? Who's doing the serving—the company or the customer? Programs and policies that cheapen the human experience are done from a place of managing the bottom line instead of the top line (the customer as depicted on the top line of my flipped org chart).

Regardless of how small or large a business, entrepreneurs need to see their businesses as mom-and-pop operations. When a business grows, it can be easy to forget about our purpose. We start focusing on profit and expansion, start pimping the details, and we forget why we got into the business in the first place. Like the television show *Cheers*, people just want to go where somebody knows their name. Even if it's a $1.4 billion company like L.L.Bean, a business needs to be treated like a mom-and-pop outfit.

Unforeseen Opportunities

No matter where you are on your road to entrepreneurship, excelling at customer service can create unforeseen opportunities. Earlier in my career, I worked as a comanager at a Wendy's restaurant. I was not particularly happy in that assignment, but I still made every effort to put my customers first. I wasn't the type of manager who stayed back in the office or even behind the counter. One morning, as I did most mornings, I grabbed a pot of coffee and walked around the dining area to refill customer cups. I smiled as I walked around, and sometimes I would even sit down with guests for a minute if they were interested in a little conversation. Among the customers one morning was a middle-aged man wearing a gray trench coat.

"Thank you," the man said as I filled his cup. "You run a good place here."

I thanked him and went about filling other cups. But about ten minutes later, he approached me while I wiped down tables. "My name's Dan Lechter." He handed me his business card. "I'm an operations director with

The Custom of Success

Grandma Gephardt's Cookie Company. I like the way you manage this restaurant and the way you interact with people. If you ever feel like making a change, give me a call."

That chance encounter eventually led to a new job opportunity—a new paid internship. Grandma Gephardt's ran a bunch of restaurants in downtown office buildings, and they gave me my first opportunity to run a store as a general manager. They also gave me a lot of leeway to try new things. It was like a trial run as an entrepreneur. But the opportunity would never have come my way if not for the high level of customer service I had been providing at my previous job.

Later when I worked on weekends as a waiter at Lorenzo's, it was again my dedication to exceptional customer service that attracted the attention of Edie Waddell. Officially, Ted Rafokolis was the owner of that restaurant, but in my mind, he was just the bill payer. I was the owner. Edie and her husband, Eric, didn't know Ted; they knew me. My job was to make sure they received the service they wanted. I can only assume they did, because they returned to Lorenzo's time and time again and always requested my table. So when I eventually ran into Edie at the McDonald's open house, she immediately saw the potential I could bring to McDonald's.

Recently, I spoke to a group of students at Southern Illinois University at Carbondale. I was picked up at the airport by Mark, a limo driver. Mark told me that he used to own a bicycle repair shop. He treated the shop as a mom-and-pop business and dedicated himself to providing exceptional customer service. One day, a customer came in who was so impressed by Mark's business that he later offered to buy it and franchise it. Mark accepted the offer.

Since he was an entrepreneur at heart, he started a transportation business while he collected payments on the franchise rights of his old business. Part of his new venture was to transport people from the airport, and again, he conducted his business with a smile on his face and exceptional attention to the needs of the customer. His level of service caught the attention of people at the university, and they eventually contracted with him to provide limousine service for dignitaries visiting the campus. His entrepreneurial career had developed and succeeded because of the satisfaction he brought to the people he served.

Remembering your purpose will keep you on track when you mess up. Excelling at customer service doesn't mean you have to be perfect. That would be impossible. But it does mean you have to be perfect at *desiring* to put your customer first. That perfect desire will guide you when things inevitably don't go right.

I wanted my employees to never hesitate in correcting a possible error. My managers and I would role-play with new employees. I would ask them, "If a customer comes back to the counter with a half-eaten Big Mac and says they ordered a Crispy Chicken Sandwich, what would you do?"

They might say, "I'd get a manager."

"No. You don't need to get a manager."

"Well, I'd tell them it was half-eaten."

"No. That's not it either. You know what you would do? You'd apologize and thank the guest for the feedback. Then you'd go to the register and refund their money and ask them if they'd like another order."

I empowered my employees to take care of our customers. Up to $20, every employee in my store was authorized to take care of their customers without hesitation. "Make it right, right away," I told them. "Deal with the customer immediately. Deal with the manager later." Employees in most businesses, however, are not empowered to make decisions because they're focused on too many policies or on a micromanaging boss. They're not focused on the customer. Not that I would encourage imperfection, but messing up can offer you an opportunity. If you handle it immediately and humbly, customers will be impressed with your customer service and return again.

The Personal Touch

It often doesn't take a lot to make a personal connection with the customer. Nor does customer satisfaction have to be at odds with efficiency. Many years ago, the McDonald's system used to call for sandwiches to be made in advanced batches. We made a whole bunch of hamburgers, for example, all made the same way, and then put them up front for customers to order. On average, we knew how many hamburgers we sold in an hour, so we could make them in advance. But the customer wouldn't know how long ago their particular hamburger had been prepared.

Then we switched to a made-for-you system. The hamburger wasn't prepared until it was ordered, and then it was prepared exactly how it was requested. McDonald's had made a smart decision because it made the order more personal, but it caused some confusion during the transition. My employees weren't used to matching up so many orders with so many customers, so sometimes our customers received the wrong order. You'll recall from those McDonald's surveys that order accuracy was the second highest customer complaint, so getting the orders right was a big deal.

Watching the ordering process one day, I came up with an idea. "Let's make it personal. We'll write each name on the receipts." Whenever a cashier took an order, she would take down the customer's name. When the order was ready, she would call out, "Mr. Jones, your order is ready." Then with a smile, she'd thank the customer personally, "Thank you, Mr. Jones."

It was a simple thing, but the customers loved it. We received so many compliments about the personalized care. I received some push-back from the corporate field people because it was outside the normal way McDonald's did things. "You shouldn't be working outside the system," they said. But then a few vice presidents paid a visit and were impressed, and I received no more push-back. They could see I had achieved two goals: I had improved order accuracy (which kept our costs down), and I had provided personalized customer service.

The longer I owned my restaurants, the more I got to know my customers. I developed true personal relationships with them. Because I tried to have my stores live up to the concept that a customer is one who develops a custom, a habit, and returns to me time after time, most of my customers were regulars. They would give me their feedback directly. "I come here because this is the friendliest and cleanest McDonald's I've ever been in." "People who work here, stay here. They know me. When I pull up to the drive-thru speaker, they know my voice. They have my three creams ready with my coffee." The approval of my customers meant the most to me. If they gave positive feedback, I knew I was on the right track.

Your customers, once they become repeat customers, will be your most important advisors. Some businesses operate on a "field of dreams" philosophy. If you saw the Kevin Costner movie *Field of Dreams*, you'll recall that Costner's character, Ray Kinsella, hears a voice telling him, "If you build it, he will come." Specifically, he is supposed to build a baseball field in the middle of his Iowa corn farm, and then people, including his father and the 1919 Chicago White Sox team, will come and use the field. Sometimes we use that as a business model: if we just build a good business and keep adding good products, people will naturally migrate toward us.

However, the world is different today. The world is flat. It's a global economy. Customers are educated. They can use the Internet to research different options. They can check features and benefits against the price of many competitors. As entrepreneurs, we have to move forward with a different mind-set. We have to get to know our customers so we can discover their problems and how we can serve as a solution.

No more "build it and they'll come." Now it's "go to them and then build." When I coach potential entrepreneurs, I encourage them to get to know their future customers by working as a paid intern in the relevant field. Then they can incorporate their suggestions when they open their business. As their business grows, they can continue to get to know the customers and develop ways to meet their needs.

Meeting needs is how we make a difference. Making people feel valued is how we make a difference. Every community craves businesses that will positively impact the people who live or work within its borders.

For me, I began to fully appreciate the difference I was making when I had to petition the city of Southfield. I wanted to open a double drive-thru, but to do so, I needed to request a permit directly from the city council. I attended the city council meeting, and when it was my turn, I addressed the council members and requested the permit. They all glanced at each other and smiled. *What's going on?* I wondered.

One of the councilmen spoke up. "Mr. Brown, we just

want you to know that we consider your McDonald's to be *our* McDonald's. We all go to that McDonald's. We appreciate what you're doing and what you add to our community through the level of service you provide." They approved the permit, and then another councilman said, "It makes us proud to help you grow your business."

A month before I sold one of the stores, a new McDonald's owner and his assistant spent three days with me, studying how I ran the store. When I met with him toward the end of his visit, he said, "It's fascinating what you've been able to do." He had seen how many people came into our restaurant and how it was a gathering point for people across the community. He had seen my employees in their white, button-down shirts and ties. He had seen the staff assisting customers while in the lobby and the dining area. "These are people who are used to getting a hamburger experience, and you've given them a filet mignon experience."

I wanted my customers to feel like they received more than they paid for. We had a dollar menu, but I

> **Freedom Thought**
>
> *Close your eyes and picture what your customer's experience will be like. Envision what will happen to make them want to return again and again. How will their experience make buying from you a habit?*
>
> *As an entrepreneur, you must strive to make an impact in the lives and experiences of your customers.*
>
> *That is your purpose. How will you exceed customer expectations? How will they be greeted and spoken to? How will you turn mistakes into opportunities? Develop your "returning customer" plan now.*

gave them a white tablecloth feeling. As a McDonald's franchisee, I couldn't control the price of the product, but I could control the value received from the meal experience. Any time a customer feels like they received more value than what they paid for, they will return. If they feel as though you're making a difference in their lives, even if it's making them feel valued for an hour at the end of a long day, they'll return.

As an entrepreneur, I wanted to always remember my purpose. My purpose was never to make a profit; that was always the fringe benefit of living in my purpose. My purpose was to make an impact in the lives of the people that encountered my business—its employees, its customers, and its community. By remembering the "why" of my ownership venture, I gave myself the freedom to make the right decisions and the freedom to succeed.

PASSION

ELEVEN
Monday Morning Heart Attack

During the early years of owning my restaurants, I hired a friend of mine to manage some of the day-to-day administrative activities. I trusted him—he was smart and loyal—and he could work part-time; I didn't have enough activity to justify hiring someone full time. He had a passion for working with inner-city schoolchildren, and that's how he spent most of his time. But he needed some extra income, so he eagerly agreed to help me out.

For the first few years, the arrangement worked perfectly. Tasks seemed to be processed on time, and he seemed pleased with the work. But as time went on, I could see his energy level dropping. He looked tired when we met, and he wasn't always fully engaged in our conversations.

Then one day he came to me and told me he was quitting. "I just don't want to do this anymore. I want to work with the children."

I was surprised. I hadn't realized the job situation was that bad—that he had been that close to quitting. But I didn't argue with him. I didn't want anyone working for me who wasn't interested in the job. So my friend showed me where all his files were located, showed me the contents of each one, and then left for good.

I was overwhelmed at first. I needed to keep up with the tasks while I searched for someone new, so the next day, I combed through the files with more scrutiny. Inside many of the folders, I found unopened envelopes. As I went through them, I uncovered notices of nonpayment and tax bills that had been left untouched. My company was behind in payments, and I had no idea.

It took me a while to learn what needed to be done, but the experience was good for me. I had left the job entirely to someone else and assumed everything would be okay. I didn't have a passion for administrative work, so I didn't want anything to do with it. I had made a mistake, and now I needed to learn some new things.

Yet I had made another mistake in addition to ignoring those responsibilities. I had put someone in charge of them who, just like me, didn't have a passion for that type of work. It was just a job to him. The more I thought about his energy levels, the more I realized he must have really disliked the job. He had done it for the money, but his heart wasn't in it. I paid for it in late fees and blemishes on my financial record.

Fortunately, other people and organizations *were* passionate about helping businesses with money management. In the long run, I needed to tap into that passion to be successful.

No Heat in the Furnace

There were no complicated reasons for my friend to fall behind in his job. He had fallen prey to simple procrastination. Procrastination grows out of a lack of passion—a lack of fire in the belly. My friend lacked a passion for his work, and he avoided doing the necessary tasks, even the simple ones. Although procrastination may be simple, it is one of the most common killers of businesses. If procrastination paralyzes a business owner, then the probability of failure will skyrocket—important tasks will be ignored, operations will lose their efficiency, businesses will look sloppy, and morale will plummet.

Earlier I told a story about Darrell who had a passion for making chicken wings but did no groundwork to determine how to build a successful wings restaurant. He had a passion, but he didn't put any practical work behind it. I've also encountered the opposite problem. I've known owners who go into business because they see an opportunity, but they have no passion for the work—they have not aligned the opportunity with the gifts and natural interests God gave them. They had started a business with a burst of energy because they had a passion for "being their own boss," but over time, the health of the business declined. The novelty of ownership wore off, and they had no passion for the specific tasks that needed to be done. They had no burning fire for their work.

Passion occurs when we set ourselves on fire and

people pay to watch us burn. People want to interact with passionate people. I stopped in a Chick-fil-A restaurant recently during a long car drive. The young man behind the counter was so full of smiles and sirs ("What would you like, sir?" and "Have a wonderful day, sir.") that he lifted my spirits and energy after a weary trip. I was so impressed by his attitude that I sought out his manager to compliment the young man. I was just passing through the town, but if that restaurant had been in my hometown, and that man's attitude was consistent throughout the restaurant, don't you think I would've returned? Sure I would have. I would have sought out that establishment on a regular basis. I would have developed a custom of going there.

People want to interact with passionate people. People *will* pay to watch you burn. To prove that, you can go to a major league sports event or watch the reaction of fans on the red carpet at the Academy Awards. We go to a sports or entertainment event to watch people who are passionate about what they do. Their passion burns through and invigorates the people watching them.

Unfortunately too many people don't follow their own God-given passions. They stand on the sideline—watching and living vicariously through others. People are desperate for the passions of others. You can see that during a sporting event when a player doesn't play with energy and desire—fans will boo him, often unmercifully. But you can also see that at Little League games—parents cheer or criticize their kids with more passion than they would ever show at work. They want to see their children demonstrating the passion that they're too afraid to show themselves. They're too afraid to burn.

Many people are stuck in jobs that don't align with their natural gifts. Several studies have determined that a higher rate of heart attacks occur on Mondays.[1] Heart attack rates are at their lowest over the weekend, and then jump 20 percent on the first day of the week. Other studies have shown that the most common time on Monday for a heart attack is between the hours of 6:00 a.m. and noon.[2] The thought of going to a job they hate is enough to kill some people.

People are vulnerable to Monday morning heart attacks because the fire is out. They're like a furnace that doesn't work; there's no heat. When you turn on the thermostat and nothing happens, you go down into the basement, the belly of the house, and check the furnace. There you discover that the gas is running, but a brush of wind has blown out the pilot light. There's no fire in the belly. The gasses of life are still flowing—opportunities are everywhere for entrepreneurship and living in freedom—but the flame of passion is gone.

---

1. O'Connor, Anahad, "The Claim: Heart Attacks Are More Common on Mondays, *New York Times*, March 14, 2006, http://www.nytimes.com/2006/03/14/health/14real.html.
2. Simeon Margolis, MD, PhD, "Having a Heart Attack: Not on a Weekend," Yahoo *LIfestyle*, September 14, 2010, http://au.lifestyle.yahoo.com/b/heartdisease/4033/having-a-heart-attack-not-on-a-weekend, accessed February 2, 2011.

Fear the Comfort Zone

Heart disease and cancer are said to be the leading causes of death in the United States, but I disagree. I think the leading cause of death is mediocrity. People die because they get comfortable—a comfortable, risk-free life seduces them, and they let their dreams die. No dream, no life.

One thing that helped propel me toward success was a deep fear of getting comfortable. Something about getting comfortable makes me uneasy. Maybe after a childhood of many evictions, I recognize that we make our own security. That when we lose the fire to improve our lives, events tend to take control of them.

Ray Kroc, the entrepreneur who built McDonald's into the world's largest fast-food business, once said, "When you're green, you're growing. When you're ripe, you rot." I believe that was Kroc's way of saying once you get comfortable, you begin to die. That's how he was able to build McDonald's from a small-scale franchise to a world behemoth. He didn't let comfort get in the way of tapping into his passion. He knew his passion would lead him to new things to learn, and he knew those new things would keep him growing and keep his business growing.

Change can be a scary thing. We're afraid of the unknown. We want to stake our claim and settle down.

When our country expanded westward during the nineteenth century, the government created land runs where they opened restricted lands to homesteaders on a first-come, first-serve basis. The most famous land run was the Oklahoma Land Run of 1889, when fifty thousand people rushed into 2 million acres of Indian territory at noon on April 22, 1889. It was a chaotic event on a massive scale. The rush for plots of land was so competitive that many people left empty-handed. The successful settlers were the ones to arrive at a plot first and stake their claim to it.

Those settlers were embarking on a great new adventure—embracing change. But we've taken "homesteading," or as I call it, "camping," to a whole new level. People rush into their careers looking for their plot to settle on. Today, that plot comes in the form of a stable situation—a situation that doesn't change—but we never find that plot because change is unavoidable. We may be able to camp in our new plot for a while, maybe even for many years, but eventually, the world changes and catches us off guard. By then our passion has died, and we're unable to respond to the changing conditions. The corporation eventually will lay us off, or assign us to some undesirable position, because our job became useless while we slept.

Some people hide from their passions because they're afraid of change. But hiding in a dead-end job isn't the only way to avoid your passion. Other people become entrepreneurs because they hate their bosses or feel obliged to follow in their fathers' footsteps, but not because they have a passion for the business they go into. In those cases, and others like them, people are still driven by fear—the fear of challenging the boss, or searching for another job, or going against others' expectations. They run away from something instead of toward something. Eventually they will fail. They won't fail because the economy is bad or they're unlucky; they will fail because they have no fire in the furnace.

Passion or No Passion—It's Contagious

The self-inflicted death of dreams doesn't just affect us. It affects our coworkers and, just as important, it affects our families. We bring our lack of happiness home with us and spread it to the people we love. Our children see that we shouldn't aspire to our dreams, and that eventually affects their desire to follow their own hopes. The negative impact of a self-inflicted death of dreams can be passed down to future generations.

Conversely, the benefits of following a passion can be passed down to future generations. In a way, I am a child of Ray Kroc's enthusiasm. Kroc was not the founder of McDonald's—that honor goes to Mac and Dick McDonald, who ran a small restaurant in San Bernadino, California. Kroc once visited the restaurant as a distributor for a milkshake multimixer and came away impressed by the fast, standardized way the brothers prepared their hamburgers. Kroc soon envisioned a chain of fast-food restaurants that would benefit from the assembly-line style of food preparation. His vision birthed a new passion, and he carried that enthusiasm with him as he acquired the franchising rights and built the company during the following decades.

To develop his business, Kroc had to recruit the best people he could find. Fortunately he had such an insatiable enthusiasm and optimism for his dream that people found it contagious. In an article titled, "Ray Kroc: A Salesman's Leader," John Baldoni states, "Ray Kroc loved the hamburger business. He could wax lyrically about the water content of french fries, or the curves of a hamburger bun. More so, he enjoyed talking up his restaurant business; it was his passion and his avocation."

I became a McDonald's owner more than fifteen years after Ray Kroc died. But I was able to fulfill my passion for restaurant service because Kroc had fulfilled his passion for a national chain of quality, inexpensive food.

Disinterest and passion are both contagious. As an entrepreneur, you *will* exhibit one or the other to your employees and customers. A disinterested owner cannot fake passion as much as a passionate owner cannot fake disinterest. Your true feelings about your business will always find a way to show through.

People who are on fire attract other people who are drawn to the fire. My friend Archie encouraged my passion to grow. For years we sat around and talked about our dreams; since he believed in me, I found that I could brainstorm ideas with him. When you're on fire, you can't have someone trying to throw a wet blanket on you. You've need people around you who are pyromaniacs—people who will find the kerosene and pour it on.

During my earlier career, I had worked at several restaurants where Mother's Day was a huge event. Customers would wait an hour or more for a table, and we would work like crazy all day long. But at McDonald's, we experienced the opposite. It was dead. Who goes to McDonald's on Mother's Day?

One day, however, Archie and I were talking, coming up with new ideas, and I wondered how we could generate more traffic on Mother's Day. Sundays usually were a huge day for us, and it would be nice to recapture some of that business.

Remember that line that Robert Kennedy used? "There are those that look at things the way they are and ask, 'Why?' I dream of things that never were and ask, 'Why not?'" Well, while Archie and I were talking, I asked, "Why can't people come to McDonald's on Mother's Day? Why can't we pack the place with customers? Maybe there are a lot of people that would like to take their mother out for a meal, but they can't afford it. Maybe we could fill a need!"

As soon as I asked those questions, I felt energy pulsing through me. I was so excited. "We could take reservations," I said. I pictured an entirely new paradigm in McDonald's service. "We'll have white tablecloths. We'll decorate the tables. We'll hire jazz musicians."

The more excited I got, the more excited Archie got.

He asked questions, offered suggestions. "Tell me more," he said. I was on fire, and Archie was my pyromaniac throwing kerosene on the flames.

By the time we finished our conversation, my passion had birthed a vision, and Archie took it and ran with it. We handed out fliers from the counter and through the drive-thru. We took reservations. All the tables were decorated, and we had musicians and a jazz singer. The tables were decorated with beautiful, floating-flower centerpieces designed by one of my employees, Miss Ivy. We made specially designed platter meals and served them on high-end Chinet plates. Every mother was handed a rose when she walked in. Archie and I worked as the maitre d's.

It was phenomenal! We marked up the prices a little to cover the added expense, but we still filled the place up. The customers ate in a McDonald's restaurant, but they received a Marriott experience. I smile whenever I think of all the families who were able to take their mothers out for dinner because of the flame of an idea that burned inside me.

Following our passion is a freedom principle. It

Freedom Thought

Passion is contagious. So is a lack of passion. Your customers and employees will feed off your enthusiasm or lack of it. As an aspiring entrepreneur, you should search your heart for what excites you. What lights you up and gives you a fire inside?

If you are courageous enough to leave the comfort zone and follow your passion, people will then follow you. They will pay to watch you burn. Make a list of everything that gets you jazzed and see how you can work those things into your business ventures.

frees us to tap into the gifts that God gave us. It frees us from the chains of the comfortable. It also encourages other people to follow us—people who are vital to our success—just like the first franchisees who were vital to Ray Kroc's success. Without passion, we are doomed to performing our tasks without enthusiasm, and like my friend, without effectiveness. With passion, we are placed firmly along the journey of success.

TWELVE
Finding the Diamonds

Mr. Weston was one of the sternest men I've ever known. And one of the kindest. He was the assistant principal of my school, St. Willibrord Catholic School. He was a tall, big white man who ran a school that was almost entirely black. He would strut through the halls each day, gripping a paddle in his hand and seeking out troublemakers. When you saw Mr. Weston rounding the corner and heading toward you, you straightened up, zipped your mouth, and did everything you could to avoid the smack of that paddle. We feared the punishment he could dish out.

We also knew something else. We knew he loved us. Every kid in that school knew that. We were his children.

Our school was near a neighborhood called Altgeld Gardens—a drug-infested housing project. Gangs had invaded the neighborhood and the nearby high school, and sometimes the gangs would hover around Willibrord to harass the children. But Mr. Weston would be outside every day—marching around, protecting us, yelling into a bullhorn, getting us into the school, and keeping the gang members away. If not for Mr. Weston—always taking command and always giving everything he had to his job—the gangs would've robbed us blind, or worse.

However, it wasn't just tough love that Mr. Weston brought to his job. He was the first person to comfort me on the day we were evicted from our first home. A neighbor had come to school and delivered the news to me while I ate lunch in the cafeteria. I raced out of the cafeteria and stormed down the hall, fighting back tears as best I could. When I neared the office, I spotted Mr. Weston consoling my brother, John.

Mr. Weston gazed down at me as I approached. His brow furrowed in a look of concern and compassion. "Your mom called me and told me what's going on," he said gently. "Everything's going to be okay."

That's when the dam broke loose. I cried. Cried hard. I buried my face in my hands and tears flowed down my cheeks and across my fingers.

Mr. Weston reached out his long arms and gathered me to him. He pressed my face against his sweater and wrapped me tight. "If you need anything at all, please let me know." He patted my back. "Tell your mother, if you need anything at all, I might be able to help."

Later I did ask him for help—specifically, I asked if there was any way I could earn some money around the school.

"Sure," he said. "You can help Mr. Christianson, the

Finding the Diamonds 145

custodian. We'll create a position for you. You'll be his assistant."

Through my remaining years at Willibrord, Mr. Weston was always respectful and treated my situation with dignity, and I always knew he watched over me. He loved me and all the children at that school, because he loved his job. He was passionate about his work and his students.

In many ways, a principal or a teacher is like an entrepreneur. Teachers, for example, have a classroom that they "own" and a "business" of educating a group of students. They often have a lot of flexibility in how they go about their "business"—the techniques they use to successfully transfer information to the consumers (i.e., students) of that information. We all can think back to our favorite teachers—the ones that made the biggest impact on our education and lives—and probably without exception, those favorite teachers were the ones who combined aptitude with passion. Their passion engaged us and captured our imaginations.

The teacher that made the biggest impact on me was completely different from Mr. Weston; that teacher was a short, little nun we called Twitch. Her real name was Sister Teresa. She was around five feet tall and walked with a limp—she kind of "twitched" when she walked down the hall.

Twitch taught high school English, and I wasn't so sure about her on the first day of school. She wasn't your typical instructor who wrote on a chalkboard while the students took notes and tried to stay awake. On that day, she announced loudly that we were going to act out *Romeo and Juliet*. We all glanced at each other with stunned and unsure looks.

"Kenneth Brown," she said, "you'll play the role of Escalus. Go up front!"

"Do I have to?" I didn't feel good that day. I had already been through a few evictions and had been sleeping on the floor of a home owned by a family friend.

Sister Teresa immediately twitched herself over to me. "Don't be a sissy," she said, grabbing my earlobe. She pulled me to the front of the room. "Be a man, Mr. Brown."

I began reading Escalus's part.

"No, no, no!" she said. "Show emotion. Get inside the character. Remember this, Mr. Brown, in this classroom our motto is: *Excellence or nothing at all.*"

I wasn't so sure about Twitch that first day, but she grew on me quickly. She brought enthusiasm to her work, and she made me love the classics. We acted out most of the works we studied, and we always had to act them out with passion in our voices. She made class fun. But she always stuck to her creed: Excellence or nothing at all. She always gave her best, and she insisted that we always give our best. I *wanted* to give my best for Twitch.

Most of us know a teacher like Twitch. Unfortunately, most of us also know a few teachers who hate their jobs. They have no passion for their work. They go through the motions and bring no joy to their tasks. What happens to the children in those classes? They act up, misbehave, and grow to dislike the information given them. A friend of mine, Tonya, once had a geometry teacher who was so cold and unenthusiastic about the subject, that Tonya finished her year hating geometry. Fortunately she moved to a different state the next year and had to retake the class. She took it from a teacher with enthusiasm, and Tonya was shocked to discover that she loved the subject; she had a real gift for it. Today she's a math teacher—passionate and enthusiastic about passing on new knowledge to her students. But if she had never had to move and been given a "redo," the direction of her life would have changed. She never would've discovered the gift she possessed.

The Fire Inside

Passion is something that comes to me from God. When I stay close to God and work on my vision, when I'm on the right track, something burns inside of me. It feels like a spirit takes hold of me, and I'm filled with energy and optimism. If I consider a business possibility, and I don't feel that spirit take hold of me, then I know that's a path I should not follow. Or if I feel a burst of initial energy for an idea, but then the enthusiasm fades, I know to be careful. Yet when an idea is on target, it won't let go of me. The passion continues to burn with the passage of time and offers a clue to the direction I should head in.

Arthur Buddhold said, "Follow your passion, and success will follow you." The opposite is also true: if you avoid your passion, success will be hard to achieve. By reading the *Wall Street Journal* and *Business Week*, you can learn about the newest trends in the marketplace, the hottest business opportunities. But success isn't some distant place you discover in the business section of your local paper. Success lies within you, comes along with you. Inspirational speaker Nancy Coey has said, "When work, commitment, and pleasure all become one and you reach that deep well where passion lives, nothing is impossible." Life is an inside job, and success happens when the impossible becomes possible. Success happens when we combine hard work with "pleasure."

To discover our passion, we must mine our hearts like a diamond dealer mines for diamonds.

Minister and orator Russell Conwell told a story in a speech he delivered around the world six thousand times. The story, called "Acres of Diamonds," tells about a man who was visited by an old priest who talked about a place where there were acres of diamonds. The man, wanting to be rich, sold his home, put his family under the care of a neighbor, and departed into the world to seek out those acres.

He searched all over the Middle East and Europe and found nothing. Eventually he arrived, destitute, at the coast of Spain. Wearing rags and feeling hopeless, he threw himself into an oncoming tidal wave and drowned.

Finding the Diamonds

After this happened, the man who had bought the home of the diamond-seeker discovered a beautiful, shiny rock on his property and placed it on his mantel as a decorative item. The same old priest eventually visited this man also, and seeing the rock, exclaimed, "Here is a diamond!"

The man who now owned the land said no, it was just a rock. But the priest insisted and proved it was indeed a diamond. They went outside and started digging and turned up more diamonds. It turned out that hidden within the dirt of the original property were acres of diamonds.

To find our riches, we don't need to search the world. We need to look inside ourselves and discover the brilliant gem, the passion, which lies hidden beneath the surface.

We can also explain this principle through what are called the three *D*s of entrepreneurial success: desire, decision, and discipline. Making constructive decisions and working with discipline are essential ingredients for success, but a burning desire is also required. How badly do you want it? How badly do you want to run a consulting business? How badly do you want to run a printing shop? How badly do you want to run the specific business you are considering (or are currently operating), and how badly do you want to do the tasks that business requires?

You'll notice that these questions are different from: How desperate are you to quit your corporate job? Or how desperate are you to be your own boss? As a business owner, you will face obstacles. Those obstacles don't arise to hold you back. They arise to test how badly you want success. They arise so you can learn new things and grow. If your desire isn't strong enough to propel you through the obstacles, then you won't learn from them, and you'll come up against them over and over again.

Within the three *D*s, decisions and discipline serve as the "adults"—those elements of success that require composed and deliberate thoughts. But desire serves as the "child" and draws us to that point where faith and passion connect. Jesus tells us that to get into the kingdom of heaven, we need to have faith "as a little child."[1] A little child believes everything is possible. A little child thinks outside the box. A little child can't contain her joy when she's excited about something. She jumps, claps, and cheers, and the adults around her get excited too. Things don't become impossible for her until she comes in contact with people who have hit obstacles and couldn't push through them.

Your Joy Meets the World's Needs

Sometimes people will ask me, "How do I know when I've found my passion?" First, I tell them about that burning feeling you should get when you follow an idea that excites you. But if they're more of a practical person, I ask them, "What would you do with your time if you didn't have to worry about money? If you were

---
1. Luke 18:17.

Finding the Diamonds

independently wealthy, where would you invest your energy?" The answer to that question often points the way to your passion. When you love something so much that you'd do it for free, and you meet the needs of others so well that they pay you, then you've found your passion. Just as money follows purpose (profits follow good customer and employee policies), money also follows your passion.

> **Freedom Thought**
>
> Make a list of all the types of businesses you would consider starting. Also make a list of all the major business activities involved in those ventures. As you review those lists, pray about each entry and pay attention to your spirit. Which ones get you excited? Which ones do nothing for you?
>
> We get our passion from God. When you stay close to God and pay attention to yourself, you'll find clues to your future success. You can learn many things after starting a business, but you must have passion from day one.

Passion leads us to our *vocation*. We usually hear about a job or career discussed in terms of our *occupation*. But an occupation is something we do to occupy our time—it consumes our time, and in exchange we get money. A vocation, as defined by theologian Frederick Buechner, is the work you are called to. The word *vocation* comes from the Latin *vocare*, which means *to call*. Buechner said: "The kind of work God usually calls you to is the kind of work that you need most to do and that the world most needs to have done. The place God calls you to is the place where your deep gladness and the world's deep hunger meet." In God's eyes, success is found at the intersection of your joy and the world's needs.

Mr. Weston found his passion when his joy for providing an education to young children met the needs of those children for knowledge and security. Ray Kroc found his passion when his joy of developing a new, creative system for preparing food met the needs of a growing middle class for dependable, fast, and inexpensive meals. I found my passion when my joy for service met the needs of McDonald's patrons who wanted to feel good about their dining experience.

I know my passion led people to my restaurants. They came once and saw my energy and excitement, and that made them feel good about eating there. Customers then returned because people naturally want to be around other people who are optimistic and enthusiastic.

Sometimes the world's needs are purely economic—cheaper food in less time, for instance. Often, however its needs are of a higher purpose. A church was located right between my two restaurants. The bishop of the church had been implementing a plan to have cell groups meet at various homes. Cell groups are smaller subgroups within the church that meet for prayer and worship. I had been involved in a cell group a few years earlier and had enjoyed the experience. When I heard about the plan of this church, I suddenly got the idea of holding cell groups at my restaurants. The idea grabbed hold of me and wouldn't let go. Why couldn't I help meet not only the need of hunger for food but spiritual hunger as well?

I went to the person in charge of the program and

Finding the Diamonds

presented my idea. At first she said no. "The groups need to be in the comfort of people's homes." But then she reconsidered and suggested that I present the idea directly to the bishop. I did just that, and he loved the idea. I was stoked!

My passion for the idea took flight. We promoted the Bible studies and prayer meetings through distributing handouts at the counter and through the drive-thru. A few people came at first, and then larger numbers. My employees would even juggle their shifts so they could attend. My passion had led me to play a part in feeding the spiritual needs of my customers. But those customers also brought people who had never been to my restaurants before. They became new customers. The money naturally followed.

When I say that the money followed (here and in previous chapters), I don't mean to sound dismissive of good fiscal management. We cannot ignore the constructive control of the money that flows through our businesses, or else it will come in one end and go immediately out the other. I learned that early on when I struggled with cash-flow issues. I was able to learn good money skills "on the job." I made mistakes and learned from them. But I could not have learned passion on the job. I had to start with that, and I had to keep it to be successful.

To experience the freedom of entrepreneurship, we must have a fire in the belly. A diamond mine of ideas lives within us, ready for the harvest.

THIRTEEN
Superman

I have a passion for public speaking. When I get up on a stage in front of a few hundred people, something happens to me. I experience an amazing connection with the audience. I feel like I'm living in my purpose when I have information that can help people live in freedom. When I'm on that stage, my juices get flowing. I'm on fire, and when people come in contact with that fire, they catch fire too. I feel like I could do anything. I feel like Superman.

I do know, in that regard, I'm not like most people. Most people don't have a passion for public speaking. In fact, they dread it. It zaps them of their strength and fills them with doubts. People who go through a normal day with confidence and composure will start shaking and sweating profusely if they have to get up in front of a group and speak. It's like kryptonite to them.

Superman understood what it meant to live in his purpose. He left his home and came to Earth, and here he realized he had physical abilities other people didn't have. He discovered a passion for helping others, and he used those abilities. But he had to stay away from the kryptonite. That was bad stuff. It could kill him if he stayed in contact with it for too long.

Passion affects us physically. To tap into our passion, we have to leave our "home," meaning we have to leave our comfort zone and take risks. If we follow our calling, enthusiasm will flow through us. On the other hand, if we avoid our passion, if we go all-in for the illusion of safety, we will also experience a physical reaction—a negative one.

The Brain Knows Passion

There is a practical reason for following your passion and not avoiding it—our bodies function better when we pursue the things that interest us.

When we fall in love, our brain releases neurotransmitters, such as dopamine. Neurotransmitters are chemicals that carry signals between a neuron and another cell. Dopamine is called a *motivating neurotransmitter*—meaning, it gets us to wake up and pay attention to something, such as that beautiful girl sitting next to us in class.

In addition to falling in love, neurotransmitters also get released when we work on a project and get "in the zone." A healthy level of those neurotransmitters gives us a sense of well-being—it makes us more productive and stable, and it fosters and encourages our creativity.

Dopamine, for example, increases goal-seeking and decreases inhibition—important ingredients for creativity. A healthy level makes us good, happy workers.

When I wake up in the morning, without an alarm clock, and I'm raring to go, those neurotransmitters are firing inside of me. They're helping me to be energetic, creative, and successful.

However, what would happen inside my brain if I had pursued a different path than the restaurant business? What if I had started a computer programming business because I had learned of the great demand for programmers in the latest and greatest programming language? Something completely different would have happened inside of me. Computer work is not one of my strong points. I'm not that good at working with numbers; I have a need to interact with lots of people. Thankfully there are many talented computer programmers who make our lives better through their work (many of their systems helped me become successful at McDonald's), but I will never be one of them.

If I opened a programming business, I wouldn't get out of bed until the alarm had gone off and I'd hit the snooze ten times. My dopamine level would be depleted. Instead of feeling energized and creative, I'd feel fatigued, irritable, and unproductive. I wouldn't succeed at my business because my creativity and problem solving would pale in comparison to someone who loved programming. Following the wrong path would serve as my personal kryptonite—sucking the life right out of me.

You can take the same Ken Brown, put him in two different situations, and he will perform differently. In the situation where he pursues his calling, he will succeed, in part because his body is programmed to help him succeed when he follows his passion. In the other, he will fail, in part because his body will suffer from the avoidance of his passion.

The Law of Momentum

The type of business to start represents just one decision in a lifetime of entrepreneurial decisions. Over a lifetime, things will change. You can count on that.

Just as developing a vision is a fluid activity (your vision will evolve over time, just as mine did), following your passion is also fluid. We may have a passion for a certain type of business for a while, but over time, that passion may fade. That is normal. Successful entrepreneurship is a journey not a destination, and we must keep ourselves attuned to our desire levels. I have talked about my preownership career as being a series of paid internships, but internships don't stop once we become entrepreneurs. The internship perspective should never stop.

I believe Michael Jordan said he knew it was time to retire when he walked through the tunnel to the court and didn't get butterflies in his stomach. Likewise, I knew it was time to start formulating my exit strategy when I also didn't get that feeling. When I attended board meetings, advertising co-op meetings, and regional leadership meetings, I used to feel butterflies just being within the orbit of all that business energy, just by breathing in the air of the arena. When that stopped happening, I knew I needed to retire before I expired.

Everything has an expiration date, a shelf life. We're just like a carton of milk. You open the refrigerator and check the expiration date on the milk. If it hasn't expired, you know it still tastes good; it's still sweet. After the date, you know the milk is turning sour; it's curdling, no longer smooth. Before our expiration date, our entrepreneurial life is sweet and smooth. But if we hang around too long, if we hang around after our passion has waned, then that life will turn sour and be filled with obstacles.

During the last year or two of my restaurant ownership, I could feel my interest waning. My McDonald's internship was nearing an end. I try to consult with other people when I'm nearing an important decision, and when I considered winding down my McDonald's ownership, I talked with a few family members. One person didn't like the idea of my giving up the McDonald's restaurants. "Why would you want to sell your children's legacy?" he asked.

I also consulted with my oldest son, Austin, who was thirteen at the time. One day I asked him, "What do you think about Dad selling the business?"

Austin thought about it for a moment, and then said, "It's a good idea."

I was a little surprised by how sure he was. "Tell me more," I said. "Why do you think it's a good idea?"

"Well, I've been watching you. I watched how you built up the business. And I've watched you lately. You don't seem as fired up as you were before. I think you're caught up in the law of momentum."

"What do you mean?"

"You know when we go to the amusement park at Cedar Point, and we go on the roller coasters? The biggest rides have a loop, but only one loop. I learned about this in school. The ride has to build up a lot of energy to have the momentum to get through the loop. Then, by the time you come out of the loop, the momentum is all gone. There's no more energy left."

"So you think I'm coming out of the loop?"

"Yeah, you were able to run the business for a while. You were able to take it to a high level. But if you stay now, it'll be anticlimatic. It'll be like the end of the roller coaster where you're just running along level track."

I smiled when Austin told me that. He understood what I was feeling exactly. He nailed it. But the person who thought I was trading in Austin's legacy didn't get it. It's my job to follow where God leads me, but it's not my job to pigeonhole my children into the path I took. The legacy I'll give Austin and his brothers is entrepreneurial knowledge, some of the money I've earned, and the encouragement to pursue their dreams regardless of whether they're similar to mine.

Pay It Forward (or Pay the Price)

I was an active member of the National Black McDonald's Operators Association (NBMOA). The association represents African American owners when they deal with the corporate entity, and it supports black owners through sharing information that would help them succeed. Occasionally the leadership committee of my chapter (the Michigan Region) would meet with black owners who were struggling to successfully operate their stores. During one meeting, we met with a gentleman who was losing money in several of his restaurants. People on the committee who knew him agreed that the owner had become complacent and had stopped managing his business with energy and enthusiasm. Still, the committee analyzed his financial records and recommended some important steps he could take to get back on track. After the meeting, I figured everything would be okay. He had a plan.

McDonald's has some tough requirements included within their franchise agreements. You have to operate your stores a certain way, and you have to give the stores the attention they deserve. If McDonald's feels like you've become neglectful, you're in trouble. That owner needed to rekindle his passion in order to get back on track. He needed to take control and become a leader again.

Passion is important for your own performance, but if you're going to be a leader, then it's important for the performance of your employees also. And the less money your employees make, the more important it is.

If an executive manages employees making $80,000 per year, for example, enthusiasm in leadership will certainly make for a well-performing team. But the higher risk factor will also motivate them. If they lose their job because the company fails, or they get fired due to underperformance, then they will face a tough challenge in finding another job at the same salary. It will take a while, and they might have to accept less pay.

People making a lower income face a lower risk. They can go to the next fast-food restaurant down the street and find a comparable job. Something else must motivate them to perform and stick around. A different level of leadership is required. If they're not getting inspired, if they're not getting motivated, if they're bored in their job, it will be easy for them to say, "Wait a minute. I'm not getting paid enough to deal with this." When a leader loses his passion for his business, that's when the tailspin begins—overall performance drops and employee turnover increases. I believe that's what happened with the owner who went to the NBMOA meeting with his financial problems.

A year later, he came back to another meeting. "I came back to say good-bye," he told me. "I'm done with the business."

"You retired?" I said. "Congratulations!"

I reached up to give him a high five, but he shook me off. "No, I'm out of business. McDonald's took it away from me. I've got nothing now."

I was stunned. He didn't know what he was going to do. He couldn't recapture his passion. That was the day I knew I couldn't let that happen to me. I had to develop an exit strategy before my passion faded. One day he had the business; the next day he didn't.

Go Out on Top

I had to be prepared for a time when I needed to hang it up and move on to the next thing. I couldn't be like one of those famous athletes who doesn't know when to walk away and stays in the game too long.

As a young boy, I remember watching some of Muhammad Ali's boxing matches. That was a man with amazing passion. I also remember his last bout, when he was thirty-nine years old. He was far past his prime and his body was far beyond the impressive physique of his youth. He lost that final bout in a unanimous decision. But Ali was far from alone in waiting too long to walk away. Most of us can probably think of athletes who didn't have the courage to retire while still at the top of their game.

> **Freedom Thought**
>
> If you're currently an entrepreneur, what is your exit plan? How will you expand your business or what new venture will you start? You don't want to become a camper—just hanging around and going through the motions.
>
> If you're just starting to consider becoming an entrepreneur, it may be too soon to plan for specific opportunities in the distant future. But it's important to remember the Law of Momentum. It's important to gauge your passion throughout your entrepreneurial life.
>
> The name of the game is to maximize opportunities. You are a climber, not a camper!

Business owners are often the same way. I sold my first restaurant for $2.6 million. That was more than any McDonald's had ever sold in the state of Michigan. It was more because most owners don't sell when they're at their peak. They hold on. Some camp out. They sell when they're desperate or all used up.

Just like an athlete, I believe entrepreneurs should leave when they're at the top of their game. I want to leave people wanting more. When I decided to sell each of my stores, people said, "Don't go." They asked me, "Why are you leaving?" I didn't get any satisfaction from letting them down. I felt bad, but eventually I would've let them down if I had stayed past my prime. The stores were ready for someone with new energy to come in and make a new impact. Most people were taught that when you arrived at the top, you had made it. They were taught that success is a destination, that the name of the game is to cross the finish line.

Actually the name of the game is to maximize opportunities—just like my mother would do when she tried to show her children glimpses of a better life. She maximized the small opportunities that came along, and that's something she taught me—keep looking for the opportunities; they'll be there. When you get to the top, you need to look for the next opportunity. When you find it, then you'll find a new and better top. Sometimes that top may be found within a current venture—some new direction you can expand into that renews your passion. But when the passion fades, then it's time to find the next opportunity somewhere else. For me, the next top came in the form of business and life coaching—helping people capitalize on their full potential.

In the business world, there's nothing sad or wrong about losing your passion. It's human. It happens. It can actually be exciting because then it's time to search for the next opportunity. I've never been more excited than I am right now. I have a vision of helping 4 million people, and I'm already on the road to achieving that goal. I can't remember the last time I was more stoked about my future.

OWNERSHIP

FOURTEEN
Destroy the Ships

What is there to say about ownership in a book about entrepreneurship? That's straight-forward, isn't it? Entrepreneurship *is* ownership. *You* own your business instead of someone else owning it. But there are two different types of ownership: external and internal. External ownership relates to the legal framework of your work situation. Do you own the finances, rights, and obligations of the business, or do you work for someone who owns those? Internal ownership relates to your mind-set. Are you the CEO of your life? Are you fully committed to your business?

In 1519 the Spanish Conquistador Hernán Cortés led eleven ships from Cuba to the shores of Mexico. On board were more than five hundred soldiers and one hundred sailors with the objective of conquering the Aztec Empire. It was a dangerous venture with much opportunity for failure—for returning to Cuba in shame. Some of the men even had divided loyalties. They talked about commandeering one of the ships and returning home. Cortés wanted his men to fully commit to the mission, so once on shore, he gave orders to scuttle all of the ships. He and his men were then stranded on land, left with only two options—victory or death.

Cortés got the commitment of his men by removing failure as an option. They were "all in." They had skin in the game—literally. They had to take complete ownership of their actions, and they did. In short time they overthrew the Aztec Empire—an empire that had stood for a hundred years.

To be successful, entrepreneurs must be "all in." We can't have one foot in our new venture and one foot back in our past life. We can't make excuses for the event failures we will face. We can't have an attitude that ultimate failure is an option. We have to be the CEO of our attitudes and our actions.

CEO of Your Life

The need for discipline (one of the three *D*s, along with desire and decision) is one of the most challenging and important traits in entrepreneurship. Our habits—how we behave in the smallest of tasks—will make or break our success. I have seen too many people go into independent business while not releasing their old way of doing things.

In Denis Waitley's book *The Seeds of Greatness Treasury*, he discusses the power of a habit. This excerpt is particularly revealing:

Destroy the Ships

You may know me. I'm your constant companion. I'm your greatest helper; I'm your heaviest burden. I will push you onward or drag you down to failure. I am at your command. Half the tasks you do might as well be turned over to me. I'm able to do them quickly, and I'm able to do them the same every time, if that's what you want. I'm easily managed; all you've got to do is be firm with me. Show me exactly how you want it done; after a few lessons I'll do it automatically. I am the servant of all great men and women; of course, I'm the servant of all the failures as well. I've made all the winners who have ever lived. And, I've made all the losers too. But I work with all the precision of a marvelous computer with the intelligence of a human being. You may run me for profit, or you may run me to ruin; it makes no difference to me. Take me. Be easy with me, and I will destroy you. Be firm with me, and I'll put the world at your feet. Who am I?

I'm Habit! [1]

Waitley illustrates not only how our habits contribute to our success but how we can influence our habits for our best interests. As Waitley wrote, "You must really be firm with me, show me exactly how you want something

---
1. Denis Waitley, *The Seeds of Greatness Treasury* (International Learning Technologies, Inc., 2003).

done, and after a few lessons I will do it automatically." You have control over your habits. In order to be successful, you have to be willing to do things you've never done before. You have to change your actions, thoughts, and associations in a way that will take you where you want to go.

Everything an entrepreneur does should be intentional. When people work for an employer, especially when those people are *camping*, they can coast through their day by just doing the minimum—responding to events as they arise and not thinking past the nose on their faces. But entrepreneurs need to think through their actions and strategically plan how they will fill their days. They need to allocate their hours in the best way to achieve success. They need to own their schedules.

When I conduct seminars, sometimes I ask the attendees, "Who here wants to own a business?" It depends on who is attending and the purpose of the seminar, but usually many of the hands will go up. "Well, guess what?" I say. "Everybody in this room already owns a business because you *are* a business. You are the CEO of your life. How you do something is how you do everything. How you do everything is your personal brand. It's how you act in this room. It's how you speak. It's how you dress. That's your brand."

As the CEO of your life, how are you managing your personal brand? What kind of clothes do you wear? How do you speak? How do you treat the people who work with you or report to you? Are you a good listener? Do you respond calmly to stressful experiences? Are you faithful? Do you tackle your work and avoid procrastination?

My experience as a McDonald's franchisee taught me about true ownership. As a franchisee, I didn't technically own the buildings or the land. I owned the restaurant *operations* but not the physical parts the business was built upon. All I really owned was the *opportunity*. I owned my service, leadership, and cash flow, and the McDonald's Corporation owned everything else. My job was to maximize that opportunity and the areas I had control over.

My greatest asset was the accumulation of my experiences. You can take away my money and the objects I legally own, but no one can take away my experiences. I own those more than I own anything else in the world. Therefore it's imperative that I make the most of them.

It's especially important to take ownership of the "bad" experiences. Life is 10 percent what happens to you and 90 percent how you choose to respond. As an entrepreneur, you can't play the blame game. You have to be like Harry Truman when he declared, "The buck stops here." You have to be like a hall of fame coach after a tough loss. He doesn't blame the players; he doesn't blame the officials; he takes ownership of the loss. He mans up and rededicates himself to learning from the experience.

Internal ownership works hand in hand with passion. My passion got me into an opportunity, and it got me through various obstacles I encountered along the way. But early on, I was over my head in certain areas of the business. During those moments, I couldn't lose my head and panic. I had to take ownership of how I behaved, and I had to learn new things.

Author and motivational speaker Tony Robbins has said, "Life is a gift, and it offers us the privilege, opportunity, and responsibility to give something back by becoming more." I believe many people would agree with this quote if it read just "privilege and opportunity," but Robbins added "responsibility." That speaks to ownership. We must own up to our responsibility to become something more—to grow and climb and not camp out.

Subject Matter Expert

One of the best ways to grow yourself (meaning to grow the business of "you") is through continuing education. You must own your knowledge and not gain it strictly by accident. The people around you—your employees, customers, and even the people in your community—will look to you to be a resource of information.

Reading is crucial for furthering your education. What you read on is what you feed on, so each year, I spend several hundred dollars on books. In addition to reading the Bible and devotional materials, I buy and read books related to my work. I have quite an extensive library, and on average, I read one book per week. I also subscribe to several trade journals.

Destroy the Ships

Most people go to college, get a degree, and then stop learning in any formal way. But college only gets you a general education. That general education is valuable at first; it gets you a job. With the passing of each year, however, general knowledge becomes less and less valuable. Who gets paid more—a generalist or a specialist? Almost always the specialist gets paid more. It's a simple matter of supply and demand; when there's less of something available—like gasoline during a hurricane—we're willing to pay more for it. So when fewer people know a lot about a specific field, they are able to attract a higher income.

When a business is known for a specific product, it's called branding. Coca-Cola and McDonald's are two of the most recognized brands in the world. They specialize in certain products and most people know exactly what those products are. You are a brand also. You are a personal brand, so what will you be known for?

In addition to mastering my habits, I committed myself to becoming a subject matter expert. I can talk to you about the food service business from the farm to the plate. I made sure I understood everything about the industry—the people, places, and things—so people could see me as representing the leading edge of knowledge. Mark Hansen, marketing coach and cocreator of the *Chicken Soup for the Soul* series, instructs people to "grow rich in a niche." One important way to do this is to grow rich in specialized information.

McDonald's did a good job of offering continuing

education classes for their store owners and employees. There was a course in Basic Shift Management, a course in Advanced Shift Management, a course in People Practices, and many others. The course load ultimately culminated in a comprehensive program called Hamburger University. Most managers and owners went all the way through Hamburger University, but most of them went no further. All the education they received was all the education McDonald's told them to get.

One time, McDonald's arranged for a local university to come in and teach a couple of courses on critical thinking. I attended the courses. The first one was held in a large auditorium that could hold several hundred people. Five people showed up. It was an optional class, so most people weren't interested in attending. It was an amazing class—one of the best I had ever taken. Since most people didn't take it with me, I increased my brand; I gained knowledge that other people didn't have.

Empty Your Purse into Your Head

To the extent you take ownership of becoming a subject matter expert—to the extent you take 100 percent responsibility for your training, for sharpening your saw—that's the extent you will grow. And the extent you grow is the extent that your staff, and ultimately your business, will grow.

How are you going to take ownership of your personal brand? How are you going to position yourself? If you take some of your profits and buy a new sports car, a thief can steal it or you can wreck it. But if you take some of that money and buy knowledge, it's yours forever. Benjamin Franklin said, "If a man empties his purse into his head, no man can take it away from him. An investment in knowledge always pays the best interest."

Entrepreneurs often think they need to have all the answers—that people need to perceive them as knowing it all. Entrepreneurs see that as a confidence issue. But being an expert isn't the same as having all the answers. I'm confident enough in myself to accept that I don't know it all. There is always more information to be gained. Motivational speaker and author Les Brown once told me, "Most people just don't know what they don't know." I've tried to remember that. Ownership means taking responsibility for the knowledge you don't possess.

Hernán Cortés faced many unknowns when he landed at Mexico and destroyed his ships. He didn't know what he would face as he and his men marched inland. But

> **Freedom Thought**
>
> *Entrepreneurs must take ownership of their habits and behaviors. What habits do you possess that work in your favor—that get you ahead? What habits do you have that drag you down—that impede your success?*
>
> *Make a list of these habits—both the good and the bad—and come up with a plan to accentuate the good ones and overcome the bad ones.*
>
> *Entrepreneurs must also determine their personal brand. How will you stand out? How will you become a subject matter expert? Develop a plan for your continuing education: What books will you read? What classes will you take? Who will you learn from? You are the CEO of your life!*

he was determined to gather information—to talk and negotiate with natives—and to use that information for his mission.

My life experience has taught me to have humility when it comes to knowledge. I want to have lots of it, but first I must recognize I still have a lot to learn. People tell me that I don't seem to have the same self-defense mechanism other people have when they receive constructive criticism. I rarely get defensive when an employee or colleague points out something about me or my business that I can improve upon. That's because I want to know what they're thinking. I believe two minds really are greater than one.

Because of the challenges I faced during my childhood—being raised by teenage parents, living through many evictions, and overcoming poverty—I learned to rely on the knowledge of others. I didn't learn to be an adversity expert by having a chip on my shoulder, by having an attitude. I learned through the knowledge other people gave me, even when they constructively criticized the way I did something.

Confident humility is important. To be a great leader, you have to be a great listener. And although it doesn't sound quite right, to be a great leader, you have to be a great follower. You have to be able to take instructions. If you're coachable and trainable, then you'll be unstoppable. You'll grow into the type of expert that attracts the attention of others and attracts success.

People can question my beliefs and philosophies.

Destroy the Ships

They can read this book and discount all the freedom principles I promote. But nobody can question my experience. I have a PhD in business. In addition to playing in the NBA someday, one of my childhood dreams was to become a doctor (they would call me Dr. K). And now I've made it to the NBA of McDonald's and earned my PhD in business experience. I didn't need a piece of paper from the Wharton School of Business to prove my knowledge. Some people pay $100,000 for a degree that's not as valuable as the experience I received. I went "all in" to learn and produce. I destroyed my ships and committed myself to "becoming more"—and got paid for doing it!

FIFTEEN
Doing What It Takes

As entrepreneurs, we need to remember our leader shadows. The shadow of a leader is a concept I taught my managers to help them remember that employees watch us—they watch us for context clues on how to behave. Good employees will listen to what we have to say, and they will do what we show them. But they'll pay the most attention to what we do when we don't realize they're watching. That gives them the most authentic information as to our core values.

When I pulled into the parking lot of my restaurants every day, I looked around to see how the lot and building appeared. One of the pillars of my McDonald's vision was cleanliness. Was trash lying around? Did the lot look dirty? One day, I drove into the lot in my Mercedes and got out. I was wearing a suit like I always did. But that didn't get in the way of my remembering my leader's shadow. I looked around and spotted a Wendy's cup that had been thrown from the neighboring lot. I also noticed some loose napkins had been dropped from the drive-thru window and had blown around the lot.

I constantly harped on the importance of cleanliness, so what should I have done about the litter? Should I have gone inside and said, "Hey, manager, why is there trash outside?" That would've gotten the job done, I suppose. The manager would have grabbed one of the workers and told him to go outside and pick up the litter. That's what a lot of owners would do. But they wouldn't be owning their shadow. Their shadow didn't pick up the trash.

I picked up the cup. Then as I walked around picking up the napkins that were blowing around the lot, one of my managers, Robert, came rushing outside with a trash bag. "Don't worry about that," he said. "I've got it covered." By seeing me picking up trash in my business suit and polished shoes, Robert knew how important cleanliness was to me. He knew it in a way that was stronger than just telling him.

The Shadow of Ownership

You cast a shadow of a leader when you treat people with respect every day. Some companies have a "people" initiative—a program to show employees how much they are valued. Some even have a "People Day"—a day to honor their employees. But people aren't a program—they shouldn't need a special effort to receive recognition. Every day is People Day when you take true ownership of your business. It's not something you do to look good in front of the media. As management expert and author

Doing What It Takes

Peter Drucker said, "Management is doing things right; leadership is doing the right things."

Leadership is ownership. Good management means we make decisions to put the right systems and policies in place that will result in a profitable business. Leadership also means we make decisions by standing on our integrity and convictions. We pick up the trash. We do what we need to do.

As I've mentioned, I do a lot of "mind talking" with myself. I have internal conversations to make sure I'm living in integrity. Before I go to bed, I look in the mirror and have a little discussion with myself. "Did you do your best today?" I ask.

I don't ask, "Were you the best today?" I usually try to be the best, but it's more important for me to *do* my best.

Then I ask, "What lessons did you learn?"

I don't have regrets. I don't beat myself up for the decisions I make. As an entrepreneur, you have to make decisions on a dime, sometimes with only a few seconds to think things over. You have to be a quick thinker, so you can't 20/20-hindsight yourself after the fact. But there are always lessons to be learned; every day brings opportunities for growth. So it's important for business owners to have those internal conversations and work through the growth opportunities that come along.

Those conversations I have with myself inevitably lead to conversations with God. As an entrepreneur, you might feel like everyone is accountable to you while you're accountable to no one. Yet everyone is accountable to his or her Maker. I believe God knows what I'm doing every minute of the day, and although I could possibly hide my thoughts and actions from my employees and customers, I can't hide them from God.

The time to take 100 percent ownership of your thoughts and actions is when things are easy. When my restaurants started taking off, some people said, half joking, half not joking, "Don't let the money change you." Or they said, "Don't let the business make you a different person." Neither money nor business ownership changes people. Instead, they amplify people—make them *more* of what they were before they started the business or came into the money. If they were trifling and untrustworthy before, they will be even more trifling and untrustworthy now.

Leaders must walk the talk. Leaders must lead by example. Leaders must remember that somebody is almost always watching them. That someone may be a business leader who wants to give you an opportunity (like the man who watched me serving coffee when I worked at the Wendy's). Or that someone may be a customer who is deciding whether to do business with you, or an employee who is trying to decide whether to do the right thing or do the easy thing.

When you walk in the sunlight, you cast a shadow behind you. That shadow does exactly what you do. When entrepreneurs lead, they stand in the light of their prominence. People naturally pay attention to them.

Doing What It Takes

When you stand in the light, what kind of shadow will you cast? The clearest example of this is at home where children watch the actions of their parents. I often see my sons mimicking something I've done without my realizing they had watched me. But anyone who follows us will look to us for spoken *and* unspoken guidance. I'm accountable to God for my thoughts and actions, but I also believe God gave me the gift of influence—the ability to positively change someone's life or situation. I have a responsibility to own that gift and to use it wisely.

Slices of PIE

Entrepreneurs take ownership by doing what must be done. Everyone wants to own a piece of the American dream. Everyone wants their slice of the pie. When I speak to young folks about leadership and ownership, I illustrate the important parts by using the acronym PIE, which stands for Preparation, Image, and Exposure. Those are the three essential ingredients for taking responsibility and control of entrepreneurial success.

Preparation

The first step in making a pie is to *prepare* the filling and the crust. You have to cut up the apples and mix them with sugar and seasonings. You have to mix the flour with other ingredients to make the pastry. In getting a piece of the entrepreneur's PIE, you have to take 100 percent responsibility for your preparation. A future leader must work toward being a subject matter expert.

I knew I wanted to own a restaurant someday, so I took paid internships at various companies in the food industry. I staked them out and learned their secrets. I gave them value, but made sure I came away understanding their systems. I needed to make sure that when the opportunity came along, I would be ready. Budding entrepreneurs need to get ready and stay ready—they need to learn everything they can, and then they need to keep their knowledge fresh. That doesn't mean you can learn everything beforehand; that would be impossible. We never learn everything. But if I hadn't learned enough to get started, if I hadn't spent time honing my skills, if I hadn't associated with people who could teach me things and serve as mentors, I wouldn't have succeeded.

We don't get out of life *what we want*; we get out of life *who we are*. When our time comes, we have to make sure we "are" the type of person who can pursue success. When it's your turn at bat, you want to make sure you can deliver. Without proper preparation, you cannot be a leader.

Image

The next step in making a pie, then, is to get the pie to look like a pie. You fill it just right. You get the crust on top to look pretty. When the pie comes out of the oven, you want people to say, "That's beautiful!" In the same way, as entrepreneurs we must ensure we convey the right image. A pie should look like a pie, and a successful owner should look like a successful owner.

In 1990 Andre Agassi appeared in an ad campaign for Canon where he uttered the infamous words, "Image is everything." Agassi took a lot of flak for the commercial because he had yet to achieve champion status in major tennis. But he eventually did, and image was an important part of his fame. I don't believe image is everything—some people take image too far and expose their superficial beliefs—but image is an important part of the entrepreneur's package.

Image is one of the most important messages I convey when I speak to students. Kids can obsess with how their image appears to their peers; they don't want to get caught dead wearing the wrong clothes or the wrong hairstyle. How they appear usually has some bearing on their social success. In the business world, however, different images prevail.

Who shows up when you show up? In order to get access to a certain world, you have to act and look like you belong there. If you want to be a CEO, you have to look like a CEO. To get access, how you dress is how you are addressed. People will respond to you based on their visual perception of whether you belong and what they think you know. As a leader, you have to set the example.

When I was serving tables at Lorenzo's, I didn't have cornrows or braids in my hair. I didn't wear earrings, and my pants didn't sag down to my thighs. I dressed like someone who could run a business. When I became a business owner, I dressed like I was a success. I wore a suit, polished shoes, close-trimmed hair. My employees could look at me and say, "That man's a success. He's worth listening to." My customers could look at me and say, "That man's a success. He's worth giving my money to." I knew that before I ever got a chance to speak to someone, I would make an impression on them based on how I looked.

If I had conformed to my friends and worn jerry curls when I went to that McDonald's open house, my future would have turned out dramatically different. If I had gone all Dennis Rodman with body tattoos, customers might have hesitated to eat at my restaurants.

One day a young man stopped in my restaurant and filled out an employment application. He was wearing cornrows. When I met with him, I told him I couldn't hire him. When I told him the reason he couldn't have a job, he accused me of discrimination. "I don't care," I told him. "I'll never hire anyone who doesn't look like he belongs here." I had my business's image to protect.

Exposure

Finally, after you've prepared the pie and made it look just right, it's time to *expose* it to the heat. To get your piece of the entrepreneur's PIE, you have to get exposure to a world of potential buyers.

In the food industry, there's a common sales tactic called sampling. When I worked for Grandma

Gephardt's Cookie Company, I never left home without having baked cookies in my possession. Every time I went to an appointment with a customer or potential customer, I had my cookies with me to expose people to my product. When I worked for Annie's Frozen Yogurt, they paid me to go to colleges, casinos, and other places to offer samples of our frozen yogurt line. They paid me top dollar to sit for seven hours and hand out stuff. When I worked for Kraft Food Services, I brought samples to all my appointments. When I worked for AWG, they sent me to colleges in a big Oreo cookie costume to hand out Oreo two-packs.

Some people look at sampling as just giving something away for nothing—a practice that hurts profits. But I see it as a practice that sows seeds. You have to expose a seed to earth and rain, you have to expose a pie to heat, and you have to expose your product to the markets and people who will make it grow.

If you want to start a Web site design business, you can offer to do a free site for a few businesses. In exchange, if you do a good job, they can promise to refer you to five other businesses. If you're an aspiring freelance writer, you can contact small, local newspapers and offer to cover an event for free. In exchange, you get your byline in the paper, which adds to your publishing credits. If you want to open a cookie business, then find a way to get your cookies out to the public before you invest in the bricks and mortar.

A budding entrepreneur named Teesha used to work for me. She made cookies and cakes, and they were incredible. She dreamed of saving enough money to open her own shop. In the meantime, she worked out of her home and handed out business cards to potential customers. She made a few sales, but not too many.

One day I asked her, "We have forty-four thousand customers coming through this place every month, why haven't I seen your cookies? Why haven't I seen your cakes? Get them in here for people to try." I told her, "Forget the business cards. Get it to the plate. If you believe in your products, then get them to the people. Don't leave home without them."

She hadn't thought of that idea. It wasn't like it was some great new idea on my part; it was just something I had seen work in other areas. She exposed her idea to me by talking about it, and I recommended she take that exposure to a far higher level. I suggested she create an order sheet and have it on hand when she handed out the samples. Her orders went through the roof. Then she took that idea and started handing out samples at trade shows. Her sales increased even more.

We have to meet opportunity halfway. Opportunity will come knocking, but we have to be at the door ready to answer. Sometimes we have to think outside the box—offering samples was a way for Teesha to be ready at the door of opportunity. As I work on this book, our country is experiencing a recession, and some people will use that as an excuse when their new business doesn't take off. But a recession means you just have to work harder at getting noticed. Money is always flowing. People aren't stashing their dollar bills under mattresses. Money is like blood in our bodies; it's always circulating. During tough economic times, it's just circulating slower than normal. But it's there for the taking if we're willing to be creative and take ownership of our exposure; if we're willing to do what it takes.

When I first started public speaking, I decided to take ownership of that new ministry, and I offered my services for free. I would go into schools and churches and tell them my vision for living in freedom. I would set them on fire! They would get so excited. Word got around, and my schedule started to fill up—exactly as I had hoped.

One day I spoke at a school, and afterward a teacher asked if I could lead one of their teacher continuing education seminars. "How much do you charge?" she asked.

Since my schedule was getting busy, I decided to throw out an amount. "Five hundred dollars," I said. The teacher agreed.

> **Freedom Thought**
>
> *Leadership is ownership. An entrepreneur must be a strong leader. Before you go to bed tonight, look in the mirror and ask yourself, "Did I do my best today? Did I take 100 percent ownership for my preparation, image, and exposure?" After tonight, keep asking yourself those questions every day.*
>
> *Change becomes harder as time moves on—complacency takes hold as you avoid risks and hard work. The challenges of owning a business will encourage your strongest habits—good or bad.*
>
> *The time to begin taking ownership is now. You are a child of God and you were made to act boldly!*

Then my schedule started filling up with $500 speaking gigs. Soon it was full, and I raised the amount to $1,000. Today schools hire me for $2,500, and I charge much more for speeches and training for other groups. But I don't think I could earn such a nice income from public speaking now if I hadn't sown the seeds early on with free speaking engagements. It earned me the exposure and reputation I needed.

In *A Return to Love*, Marianne Williamson said, "Our deepest fear is not that we are inadequate. Our deepest fear is that we are powerful beyond measure. It is our light, not our darkness that most frightens us. We ask ourselves, Who am I to be brilliant, gorgeous, talented, fabulous? Actually, who are you not to be? You are a child of God. Your playing small does not serve the world."[1]

The fear of failure is an enormous problem. I've talked with many people who tell me they've got a great idea. "But I'm so nervous," they say. "What if nobody likes it?" They hide their idea in the dark—away from exposure, away from the possibility of failure. That's not leadership. That's not taking ownership. That's not doing what it takes. That's giving up. That's abandoning a dream, giving it away for nothing. Everybody is a child of God, and playing small does not serve the world or the person with the dream. Entrepreneurs must be bold.

If you open a cookie and cake store without first

---

1. Marianne Williamson, *A Return to Love: Reflections on the Principles of a Course in Miracles* (New York: HarperCollins, 1993)..

Doing What It Takes

exposing your product to potential buyers, then you dramatically increase the risk of failure. If Teesha had received mixed reviews from the people who tasted her samples at McDonald's, she would've had time to make adjustments in her product without the pressure of paying rent or employees. Without the advantage of sampling, she might have opened her store to mixed reviews, and that would've been the kiss of death—for the store and the dream.

Leadership and living in freedom require that we take risks. We need to expose our dreams to people (the right people, not the naysayers) who will help us grow them into something real. Ownership means we have a responsibility to our dreams—we owe them something; we owe them the opportunity to see the light of day.

Doing what it takes does not mean we do everything. Entrepreneurs must live balanced lives (which I'll address in the next chapter), and we cannot get sucked into micromanaging all the activities of our business. There's no freedom in running ourselves ragged. But when leadership is called for, when preparation, image, and exposure are called for, entrepreneurs must conquer fear and take ownership.

SIXTEEN
A Balanced Life

It took a few years of owning my restaurants before I learned what ownership was really all about. During those first years, I worked very long hours. I was the rat running a race on a treadmill. I got up at 4:30 a.m., had my devotional time, and then darted off to work. On the way I picked up donuts and fruit for the staff, and still I arrived at the restaurant before anyone else. I took pride in being the first one there. I even put myself on the schedule as the opening manager. My faith in my systems was strong, but my faith in my people wasn't.

After the staff ate breakfast, I'd gather them for a shift huddle. I'd give them their assignments and our goals for the shift, and then we were off. Lights, camera, action! I rode the adrenaline of our operations all day. I did everything. I worked the drive-thru. I counted down drawers. I ran to the bank. I placed orders for supplies. I trained. But I never stepped outside the frantic pace of the day to see how we were doing strategically. That's when I got into some trouble with cash flow and taxes. I had taken ownership of the business at the ground-floor level, but I hadn't taken ownership at the strategic level.

After a busy day, I got home around 10:00. My wife had left my dinner on the stove. I ate it quickly, kissed my boys good night while they slept, and crawled into bed. Then it started all over again the next day, like I was living in the movie *Groundhog Day*. Adrenaline kept me going for a while without adequate sleep, but it started to take a toll on my well-being. I got sick more often and was more irritable. I loved being an owner and immersed myself into every aspect of my restaurants. I was hands-on and energetic—always willing to jump in and run the counter or the fryer, if needed. But I wasn't on top of things. I was the player on the field constantly chasing after the ball, instead of the coach on the sidelines, strategizing and managing.

Spinning the Plates

I needed to learn that freedom in entrepreneurship requires a balanced life. You have to take ownership of all aspects of your day-to-day existence.

Now when I start a coaching relationship with entrepreneurs, I send them a questionnaire to fill out. One of the most important questions I ask is: *How much of your life do you own*? Through that question, I mean to provoke some thought about how much of their day is spent doing the right things and in the right way. True entrepreneurship is about taking ownership of all parts of your life. It's about balance. If you could slice up your life like a pizza, how big a piece do you slice out for your business? How big a piece do you give to your family? How big a piece to your spouse? How big a piece to your spirituality? Your community?

A great many entrepreneurs give almost all of their pizza to the business. They own their businesses, but they rent their families and spirituality. The important pieces outside the business are not integral parts of their lives.

I lost some friends and family members because I was so focused on selling food. I believed the world would evaluate me based on only one thing: sales. Within two years of buying the store at 10 Mile and Telegraph, I had already increased sales by 20 percent (I would increase them by 70 percent within five years). That, to me, seemed like success. But I was running out of steam. I was getting burned out. What kind of success would I be if I couldn't keep up the pace indefinitely? What kind of success would I be if I hit a brick wall and had to quit?

I spoke with my business coach and asked for his advice. How could I keep up the pace? Instead of answering immediately, he asked me a few questions. "Ken, when was the last time you took your wife on a date?"

"Well," I stammered, "I'd like to. I just haven't had a spare moment."

"When was the last time you showed up at your son's

baseball game? When was the last time you went to church?"

"Not in a while," I admitted.

We talked some more, but he had made his point. I was exhausting myself because I hadn't lived a balanced life.

An entrepreneur is like the guy at the circus who keeps a bunch of plates spinning on thin rods. If he just focuses on one plate, constantly spinning with intensity, then he's going to end up with a lot of broken plates. All but the one plate will crash from neglect. Eventually the one that's being intensely spun will also fly off and crash. No, a plate spinner only succeeds by paying balanced attention to all the plates.

Entrepreneurs who focus too much time on their businesses often deal with health problems, such as high blood pressure, heart disease, and obesity. Eventually those health problems make it difficult for them to enjoy the fruits of their labors. In his book, *When the Game Is Over, It All Goes Back in the Box*, John Ortberg tells the story of a man who worked hard at his career. He amassed many of the symbols of success. Because he worked so hard, he was usually still working at his computer when his wife went to bed. One night, his wife got up during the middle of the night and saw him slumped in his chair, asleep. She decided to let him sleep and not wake him.

In the morning, however, she checked on him again and discovered he wasn't asleep. He was dead. He had

A Balanced Life

died working and couldn't take the fruits of his labors with him.

When the game was over, everything went back in the box. Ortberg asks:

> *A fantastic career, a new house, a plush 401K, a secure retirement, good, all good. But what is it all about? No matter how skillful you play or how many tokens you acquire, a time arrives when the game of life comes to an end. Now what? Now it all goes back in the box. No more games, no more card games, no more tokens, no more emotions, no more financial planning, no more RVs, no more vacation homes, the game is over. What do you win that you get to keep?*[1]

The man in this story didn't truly own his possessions (he had to leave them behind). And he didn't own his life; he gave it up. He sacrificed his health and his family because he couldn't step away from his business.

Melody Beattie has written several books to help people trapped in codependency, such as people who get emotionally consumed by a loved one who has an addiction or is depressed. Entrepreneurs sometimes have similar traits to people who are codependent—their business can't seem to live without them, and they can't

---

1. John Ortberg, *When the Game Is Over, It All Goes Back in the Box, Participant's Guide: Six Sessions on Living Life in the Light of Eternity* (Grand Rapids: Zondervan, 2008).

seem to let their business go for even a few hours.

In *The Language of Letting Go*, Beattie writes, "A balanced life has harmony between a professional life and a personal life. . . . Just as a balanced nutritional diet takes into account the realm of our nutritional needs to stay healthy, a balanced life takes into account all our needs: our need for friends, work, love, family, private time . . . [and] time with God."[2]

Delegating Like Moses

We have needs beyond the demands of work. We can't be all things to all people. Being all things might feel like ownership, but it's not. When the fire chief is up front with the hose, then events are directing him instead of him directing events. Ownership is about stepping back, relying on other people, and striking a healthy balance in your life.

I liked to be visible in my restaurants. Customers would come in, and if they had an issue with something, they would come to me. They wanted the Grand Poobah. They would look past my crew and my manager and say, like Uncle Sam, "I want you!"

Because the business was my baby, I wanted to be the one who always fixed things. But I was disrespecting my crew and managers by doing that. I was sending a message to them that I didn't believe they could fix things and that they didn't have the authority to do

---

2. Melody Beattie, *The Language of Letting Go* (Center City, MN: Hazelden Publishing, 1990).

so. I unraveled the training I had invested in them. So, although it was counter to my instincts, I learned to take real ownership, and I let my staff handle most things. When a customer approached me with an issue, I said, very graciously, "I don't handle that. But you can go to Robert (or whomever), and he will take care of whatever you need."

Delegating more decision-making responsibility to my staff aligned with my *people first* philosophy. Employees should be stretched and not compressed. Their growth should be encouraged, and to do that, sometimes we need to put our success at risk.

I once heard of an experiment that used a dog to demonstrate how animals can be trained to self-limit themselves. They put the dog on a leash, and then set down a bowl of food just out of reach. The dog would stretch and stretch for the food, but he couldn't get to it. The leash tugged on his collar, practically choking him, and still the dog yearned for the food, extending his body as far as it would go. The dog quit trying for a while, and then later, went back to reaching for the food. He quit trying once again, and gradually, the times of giving up grew longer and longer until the dog gave up for good. The experimenters then loosened the leash, but the dog never attempted to get to the food again. He had been conditioned to believe he couldn't reach it. He had given up ownership of his fate. If he had lived in the wild, he would have starved to death.

Successful entrepreneurial ownership requires that

the people supporting us take ownership also. We need to put demands on the potential of our employees. When they take ownership along with us (instead of us micromanaging them), our business will only benefit. By stretching the expectations of those supporting you, they will win, your customers will win, and ultimately you will win.

I realized I couldn't keep a healthy balance in my life because I wasn't delegating activities. I was a problem solver, and I ran around trying to solve every little problem that popped up. I micromanaged. I was like Moses trying to solve all the problems of his people when they were in the wilderness. From morning until night, the Israelites would come to Moses with their problems.[3] They would have dilemmas or disagreements, and since Moses knew God's laws and statutes better than anyone, he was the obvious person to turn to.

But Moses' father-in-law, Jethro, observed how hard he was working and knew it was a problem. "What is this you are doing for the people?" Jethro asked. "Why do you alone sit as judge, while all these people stand around you from morning till evening?"

Moses told him why. Someone needed to settle the disputes.

But Jethro said, "What you are doing is not good. You and these people who come to you will only wear yourselves out. The work is too heavy for you; you cannot handle it alone."

---

3. See Exodus 18:13–26.

A Balanced Life

Jethro instructed him to:

> *"Teach them the decrees and laws, and show them the way to live and the duties they are to perform. But select capable men from all the people—men who fear God, trustworthy men who hate dishonest gain—and appoint them as officials over thousands, hundreds, fifties and tens. Have them serve as judges for the people at all times, but have them bring every difficult case to you; the simple cases they can decide themselves. That will make your load lighter, because they will share it with you. If you do this and God so commands, you will be able to stand the strain, and all these people will go home satisfied." (Exodus 18:20–23, NIV)*

That was one of the earliest examples of delegating. Jethro essentially told Moses to rely on his shift leaders, assistant managers, managers, and division managers ("officials over thousands, hundreds, fifties, and tens"). Moses needed to train them right, and then trust them. The tough decisions could still come to him, but otherwise, he needed to delegate. That would be the only way to survive.

An entrepreneur's efforts should be targeted. We need to do what it takes to achieve success (as I discussed in the previous chapter), but we don't need to do everything.

If there's no way to succeed other than working ninety hours a week, then we have not set up our business in a systematic way.

I had learned the value of systems through my experience before my McDonald's ownership. SYSTEM, you'll recall, can be an acronym for Save YourSelf Time, Energy, and Money. I needed to have a process in place for most decisions, and then I needed to rely on my people to take care of things. I needed to respect them by trusting their problem-solving abilities, and I needed to encourage their growth by letting them handle more of the decisions.

When you get systems in place—for opening the store, for handling dissatisfied customers, for paying bills, for placing orders, for almost everything—then you don't have to direct people that much. You can still lead them, but you can work *on* your business instead of *in* your business. By delegating, you can take your head out of the sand, look around, and see what's going on with your business in the big picture. You can make strategic decisions better because you're not exhausted, and you can balance your life better—paying more appropriate attention to your family, friends, spirituality, and community.

Pulling Away

I had to take ownership of my balanced life by occasionally unplugging from my ownership of the business. I couldn't always stay connected. That goes against conventional wisdom for an entrepreneur. The images we have of successful entrepreneurs are of people with unlimited energy who always have a cell phone to their ear. They prove their dedication to their business by remaining connected to it at all times. I eventually resisted this compulsion and proved my dedication to my business by sometimes pulling away.

When I went home at night, I turned off my phone. On Sundays I would leave it off all day. At first it was very hard for me to feel like a leader and not answer calls. But something happened when I let those calls go into voice mail. My staff had been calling for every little thing, which was natural because I had encouraged that through my intense involvement. When I didn't answer and didn't call back, they were forced to make decisions. And guess what? The building didn't burn down. Food got served. Customers went away just as happy as they did when I was there. That built up my staff's confidence, and it built up my confidence in them. I had trained them and set up the necessary systems. I needed to step back and let them use that training and those systems so I could conserve my energy for the long haul.

My time away from the business gave me more time with my family. I attended more of my boys' sports events, and I took my wife out on more dates. I also got away by myself. Every three months or so, I unplugged from everyone for a few days. I recommend all entrepreneurs do the same thing. As an entrepreneur, a lot of people—your customers, employees, suppliers, family members—want something from you, and you need to get to a place where no one wants anything. It doesn't need to be an exotic place. It could be the Super 8 Motel. Just as long as you're by yourself and you're not electronically connected to your business. As I mentioned in the section on faith, I like to unplug so I can connect with God—so I can plug into the Source of life. I follow the model that Jesus used; he always found time to go off by himself for time with his Father. When I get away, I bring my Bible and my devotional books with me, and I spend quality time with God. I also read other books from my library—books on success, entrepreneurship, motivation, and business.

Whenever I planned to get away, I put the dates on my calendar. That helped me prepare to be away and stick to my plan. I also put it on the calendar at work so my staff would know I wouldn't be available. After a while they learned not to bother calling when I wouldn't be available. Eventually I could be at home, just a few miles from work, with my cell phone on, and no one would call. People thought I was too busy when I wasn't available, but I was the opposite of busy. I was sharpening the saw, recharging my soul and my energy. When I returned from unplugging, I was vibrant and creative.

Managing my calendar played an important role in my taking complete ownership. I used to fill my calendar with business activities, and then I slipped my family into my life like an afterthought. But when I decided to

A Balanced Life

pursue complete ownership, I recorded my family and spiritual time on my calendar first. I got their schedules and transferred them over to mine. Then I worked business activities around a lot of what they had going on. If my son had a game, it went on the calendar. If I needed to take my wife out on a date, I put in on the calendar. If I needed a private sabbatical away from everything, I put it on the calendar.

During my off-hours, I also returned to some of the hobbies I loved before I became an entrepreneur. I already mentioned my love of reading. But I also enjoy bike riding and listening to jazz music. As part of taking ownership of my life, I would go to Borders and find a chair and read for a few hours, take bike rides around the neighborhood, and go to jazz concerts.

Many entrepreneurs I talk with don't participate in a hobby. They'll tell me golf is their hobby, but I'm sorry, golf is not a hobby. Exchanging business cards and striking deals while chasing a little white ball is not a

> **Freedom Thought**
>
> *An entrepreneur must live a balanced life to achieve true success. What is out of balance in your life? What "plates" are you ignoring? Which ones do you focus on too much? Take a close look at how much time you put into your business activities, family, spirituality, and community.*
>
> *Starting a business might consume a lot of hours, but in order to succeed over the long haul, we must eventually balance things out. You must periodically unplug from the business. And you must invest energy into other areas of life you find enriching.*
>
> *If you are an aspiring entrepreneur, then develop a plan now for living a balanced life.*

hobby. Entrepreneurs need to be involved in activities they love that have nothing to do with their work.

When people are highly successful at business but don't have balance in their lives, I'm not impressed by their success. If business is all you focus on, you should be successful. You *should* be the number-one salesperson if you're not home with your family. You *should* be raking in the dough at your business if you're missing out on your child's life. If you haven't burned out yet, then you should be a financial success. That's a given. There's nothing special about that.

However, if an entrepreneur's wife says, "Not only is my husband a wonderful provider but he still takes me on dates and buys me flowers. He's fully engaged in the household," then I know he's a *real* success. If his child says, "My father coaches Little League. He's busy with his business, but he usually finds a way to coach my games," then I know he's a *real* success.

We can't achieve freedom by running in the rat race. Real success, real freedom, comes when we take complete ownership of every part of our lives.

ASSOCIATIONS

SEVENTEEN
Iron Sharpens Iron

In the movie *Facing the Giants*, a football coach tries to inspire his team to succeed beyond their expectations. One of the leaders on the team, Brock, talks about another team, saying there's no chance of beating them. The coach calls Brock out on the field to do a death crawl—an exercise where another player climbs on Brock's back (back-to-back), and Brock must crawl fifty yards while carrying the other teammate. The coach makes Brock promise to do his best and not give up, then the coach blindfolds him.

Brock, laboring under the weight of his teammate, starts out at the end zone line and heads for the fifty-yard line. Brock must crawl on his hands and feet without letting his knees touch the ground while keeping the other player balanced on his back. The camera zooms in on Brock, and we see the intense concentration in his face. The coach constantly yells at Brock—not to give up, to keep going, to give his best with every step. And he encourages him. Brock's coach is his advocate and cheerleader, driving him toward that fifty-yard line. The farther he goes, the weaker Brock gets, and the more he wants to give up. But his coach won't let him. "Just thirty more steps!" he yells. "You can do it!" Finally Brock arrives at the end and collapses. The coach removes the blindfold and tells Brock, "You're in the end zone." He had crawled, carrying a teammate on his back, for one hundred yards, not just fifty. The coach had pushed him to achieve twice what he thought he was capable of doing.

As entrepreneurs, we carry a lot on our backs. We carry our families and their financial security. We carry our employees and their financial security. We carry the satisfaction of our customers. We carry our integrity and reputations. To survive and thrive, we need to associate with people who will encourage us, believe in us, and push us to excel. Will Rogers said, "A man only learns in two ways, one by reading, and the other by association with smarter people." I've already discussed the importance of reading in my life, but the influence of the people in my life is just as important.

The coach's influence made Brock achieve a level of success he thought was impossible. But it would not have happened if a naysayer had walked alongside him and yelled. If the screamed comments were, "You can't do it!" and "It's impossible!" would Brock have crawled one hundred yards? Absolutely not. Would he even have crawled the original goal of fifty yards? Probably not. The influence of the person in close proximity to Brock made an enormous difference.

Not by Yourself

Our associations can add to our freedom or take it away. The Law of Associations says we become the top five people we surround ourselves with. There's a significant benefit to associating with powerful, passionate people. Proverbs 27:17 says, "As iron sharpens iron, so a man sharpens the countenance of his friend." Other people, the right people, can make you sharper and stronger. Being an entrepreneur can be a lonely existence sometimes. You don't have any counterparts within your workplace. If you're a manager in a corporate office, there are usually other managers to commiserate with. You can meet in the break room and share your triumphs and struggles with each other; you understand each other. You can also meet with your boss and other higher-ups and learn from them. If you're fortunate to work for a good boss, he or she will mentor you and guide you in your advancement. But as an entrepreneur, you will rarely find opportunities for commiseration and mentoring within the workplace. You have to be intentional and go outside for that influence.

The book of Ecclesiastes says: "Two are better than one, because they have a good reward for their labor. For if they fall, one will lift up his companion. But woe to him who is alone when he falls, for he has no one to help him up. . . . Though one may be overpowered by another, two can withstand him. And a threefold cord is not quickly broken."[1] Many businesses fail because

---
1. Ecclesiastes 4:9–10, 12.

the owners see themselves as an island unto themselves. If they are sole owners, they say, "I'm in business for myself. I don't have anyone else to rely on." But in the franchise world, there's a saying that goes: "In business for yourself, but not by yourself." Franchises have many pros and cons, but one of the upsides is the support structure that is often put behind you. However, people can find a support structure even in entirely independent business ventures.

The first step in finding support is to make sure you look for the right kind of support. Too many entrepreneurs surround themselves with *yes men* but not people who will be honest and speak up when you head down the wrong path. When you look at Michael Vick, Tiger Woods, or any number of corrupt politicians, they most likely didn't associate with peers who would hold them accountable to the right decisions.

When an entrepreneur surrounds himself with yes men, it gives him an ego boost. He feels like hot stuff. He feels like he knows it all. But that's just a trap for a downfall. An old saying goes: "You can't give a big vision to a small mind." Small minds won't know how to help your vision manifest itself. They certainly won't know how to make your vision grow into something even bigger and better. They end up sabotaging your dreams.

Early during my McDonald's ownership, one of my supervisors struggled with being a yes man. Almost every day I sat down with him for strategy sessions. I downloaded my vision to him—my mission, my purpose, my passion—and then his job was to download it to the managers. That seemed to work all right. But after a while, I realized I felt a little annoyed with him when we spoke. I didn't feel an adequate level of respect for him, and I realized the reason was, he would never say no to me. He would never question what I wanted to do. As visionary leaders, we need to have people around us who will constructively challenge our ideas. People who will push us, who will say, "I respectfully disagree and this is why . . ." Without those types of people, we are at a greater risk of having our mistakes exposed to the world.

The Emperor's New Clothes

Yes men are not in your best interest. Do you remember Hans Christian Andersen's story about "The Emperor's New Clothes"? As the story goes, there was once an emperor who was obsessed with clothing and looking good. He had a grand vision of how he should look. One day, two swindlers came to town and told the emperor they could make him new clothes from the finest silk. The material had a special property, however. It would be invisible to anyone who was stupid. The emperor agreed to have the clothing made for him, since he thought it would be a good way to identify the fools in the kingdom.

The swindlers started "making" the fabric on a loom. The emperor was anxious to find out what it looked like, so he sent his most trusted and honest minister to check it out. The minister couldn't see the fabric, but he was so embarrassed, he told the emperor what he wanted to hear—that the fabric was beautiful. The emperor then sent a second advisor, and he reported the same details back to the emperor.

Well, you probably remember the rest of the story. The emperor, trusting that his advisors could see the fabric, put on the new set of clothes, and then paraded naked before the kingdom. His subjects all commented on how beautiful the fabric was until a child, too young to be a yes man and tell the emperor what he wanted to hear, called out, "But he hasn't got anything on!"

The emperor's yes men destroyed the emperor's vision of how he should look before his subjects. Their yeses humiliated him. In a way, yes men will leave an entrepreneur naked—unprotected against the flaws in his plan and undirected in the best way to proceed.

Through my experience as an entrepreneur and my experience as a coach, I've noticed that first-generation business owners can be more prone to hire yes men than second- or third-generation owners. Mick Asmussen, for example, was the third generation owner of AWG—a company I once worked for. His grandfather had made handshake deals with several clients during the early years. During the course of several decades, he had built trusting relationships with customers, suppliers, and especially support professionals. When Mick took over the business, his grandfather and father had developed deep relationships with accountants, attorneys, and other professionals. Those people weren't just hired off the street by Mick. No, they were family.

First-generation owners can fixate on wanting things to work exactly as planned, and they fear someone raising issues with that plan or suggesting a different route. Those entrepreneurs get emotionally invested in not only their broad vision but the exact details working out perfectly.

One time early in my McDonald's ownership, my lawyer strongly recommended taking a course of action that I disagreed with. I was very tempted to fire him over the disagreement. *How dare he hold such an opinion,* I thought. I was locked into my way of thinking, and I didn't know him well enough to trust his judgment. If Mick's lawyer disagreed with him, however, Mick wouldn't even think about firing him. First of all, the trust level was too high, and Mick would respect his opinion. And second, if Mick threatened such a thing, the lawyer would probably get Mick's father involved in the dispute.

As first-generation entrepreneurs, we don't have those "family" relationships to rely on, and we can't develop them overnight. But Mick's grandfather did develop them, and that should be our goal as well. Developing those associations will pay big dividends down the road.

The Mastermind Group

Think about the people you are close to. Every single one of them has an impact on you. They either add, subtract, multiply, or divide your life. No one in your close inner circle is neutral. Well-meaning people will subtract from us by trying to protect us—by discouraging us from pursuing our dreams and reminding us of the possibility of failure. Other people may divide us by actively working against our dreams. Those are the types of people we need to remove from influencing us, and if they are involved in our business in any way, we must literally remove them from that involvement. The people we need are the ones who will add and multiply—add through encouraging us and multiply by actively helping us.

Napoleon Hill, in *Think and Grow Rich*, introduced the concept of a mastermind group—a concept that was inspired by the steel magnate Andrew Carnegie. Have you ever noticed how wealthy people tend to hang out together? There may be various reasons for this, but one reason is that successful, creative people feed off the success and creativity of others. They acknowledge that each individual doesn't have all the answers, and they can be stronger through the influence of other similarly driven minds.

Carnegie formed a mastermind group with approximately fifty men—business associates he surrounded himself with in order to advance the production of steel and Carnegie's business ventures. According to Hill, Carnegie "attributed his entire fortune to the power he accumulated through this 'Master Mind.'"[2] Together, the group formed a collective "master mind," an intelligence

---
2. Napoleon Hill, *Think and Grow Rich* ( ), .

that was fifty times greater than any one person.

Carnegie's group was formed for a very specific purpose, but you can also form a mastermind group of diverse business leaders for the purpose of sharing resources, feedback, accountability, and creativity. One person might excel at finance. Another at marketing, another at legal issues, and yet another may simply be a highly inventive person who is always thinking up ideas. It's not that hard to form a mastermind group. Basically, you reach out to two or more people in your network, people like you (owners, peers within supplier organizations, etc.), and ask them to be part of a group to share ideas and offer advice. Most people feel honored to be asked. You can meet periodically in person or informally over the phone or the Internet.

A mastermind group is a network of people who are on equal footing. It's a small group of people whom you trust, and respect, and whose opinions you value. As a group, they mastermind you. Napoleon Hill said, "No two minds ever come together without, thereby, creating a third, invisible, intangible force which may be likened to a third mind."[3] It's this third mind where the whole of the group's thoughts and advice are greater than the sum of the parts—greater than your individual thoughts and ideas. The mastermind gives you a new way of thinking. Out of those groups come great ideas, and sometimes even formal alliances and funding, but it's the collective brainstorming where the most frequent value lies.

---
3   Ibid, .

Talking about Dreams

A mastermind group can be as small as two people, but personally, I believe it shouldn't be much more than twelve. A twelve-person group is a good size and worked well for the disciples of Jesus, but if the group gets too big, it becomes challenging to manage. You want a group of people with whom you can be vulnerable. For example, if you're considering a decision that may or may not cross an ethical line, you want people who will not judge you, but will allow you to talk things out while holding you accountable to the right decision.

The people in a mastermind group may have different backgrounds and expertise, but you want one thing in common. You want everyone to be out-of-the-box thinkers. You don't want any fly-by-night dreamers—people who are all talk and no action—but you want upperly mobile, progressive thinkers who like to act on their dreams and encourage the implementation of other people's dreams.

I have twelve people in my mastermind group. They have similar entrepreneurial minds, but they also have valuable differences. For example, in my group is a university professor who is very entrepreneurial-minded, but also is structured and cerebral; an entrepreneur and author who also passed the bar exam without actually going to law school; and a man who has started about six businesses in the last fifteen years.

As a business and life coach, I now organize and lead

other mastermind groups. I bring entrepreneurs together to talk about their issues and learn new things. I bring together people from all over the country, and we utilize a bridge phone line to have our meetings. I assign books to the group—books like *Good to Great*, *The E-Myth*, and *The Millionaire Next Door*, plus some of my books. We read the books during a common time period, and then discuss them together. *What principles did we learn from the most? What are some new, practical steps we can take that respond to those principles?* The group discussions offer a chance to brainstorm the collective entrepreneurial mind and see what ideas bubble up.

In *The Law of Success*, Napoleon Hill tells the story of Dr. Gunsaulus, a young preacher who was scheduled to preach in Chicago one Sunday. He put ads in the Chicago newspapers giving the title of his sermon: What I Would Do If I Had a Million Dollars! The advertisement caught the attention of a wealthy entrepreneur, Philip Armour, who decided to attend the service.

Freedom Thought

Entrepreneurs are not in business by themselves. Even if they run a solo operation, they need to surround themselves with friends and associates who are supportive and honest. You need people who will encourage you, but not people who are yes men.

Make a list of all the associates you could include in a mastermind group.

Your mastermind group should include people with entrepreneurial spirits and out-of-the-box thinking. You can get together in person, over the phone, or even on the Internet.

Take the initiative. Get in touch with those people and get the group going.

In the sermon, the preacher talked about the need for people to learn how to think in practical ways—that theoretical thinking only got people so far, and we needed practical know-how to reach success.

If he had a million dollars, the preacher said, he would open a school of technology that would teach young men and women how to succeed in life by thinking in practical terms—a school where students would "learn by doing."

Mr. Armour attended the service and was impressed by the preacher's vision and passion. After the service, he walked down the aisle to introduce himself. He told Dr. Gunsaulus, "Young man, I believe you could do all you said you could, and if you will come down to my office tomorrow morning I will give you the million dollars you need." Later, Gunsaulus would form the Armour Institute of Technology with Mr. Armour's financial backing.[4]

I'm an optimist by nature, but not enough of one to think we can just start talking about our dreams and a stranger will walk up to us and hand us a million dollars. We do need to put ourselves in position to associate with the right people—good people who can help us on our entrepreneurial journey.

In that story, Napoleon Hill said, "There is always plenty of capital for those who can create practical plans for using it."[5] Entrepreneurs have dreams, but it usually takes other people to help turn those dreams

---

4. Napoleon Hill, *The Law of Success* ( ), .
5. Ibid, .

into reality—it takes people with practical knowledge to get beyond the theoretical visions. Henry David Thoreau said, "If you have built castles in the air, your work need not be lost; that is where they should be. Now put the foundations under them." One of the best ways to build those foundations is through the knowledge and support of others—through the associations we make.

EIGHTEEN
Soaking Up Knowledge

We can find the people for our entrepreneur's network from many sources. Although family members can sometimes be discouragers, other family members can be our biggest fans. My mother and father, for instance, believed strongly in my potential for success and pushed me to pursue my dreams as far as they would carry me. As aspiring entrepreneurs, we can look around our family and close friends to see who might be able to support us.

When I look back, I realize the entrepreneurial spirit has always been in my blood. My grandfather owned a restaurant many years ago in Tampa, Florida. Then my Uncle Sonny opened several businesses while I was growing up. He owned a clothing store, an ice cream parlor, and a hamburger stand. When I was thirteen, I worked occasionally at Sonny's hamburger stand, Fat Men Double Deckers, and I got exposure to the inner workings of a small business. My father and grandmother worked there, and on weekends I bussed tables.

Later, as an adult, Chuck Goldberg became my mentor. He helped run a family business, AWG, a food broker and distributor. I worked for Chuck for several years, and through that experience, I learned about operating a larger business. And when I worked for Sysco, I sold food to Charlie Robinson who owned four Charlie Robinson's Ribs restaurants. He was a shrewd entrepreneur who managed his money tightly. Although it took some time to earn his trust, he eventually became another mentor for me—someone who taught me about operating multiple restaurants.

Through our family members, friends, and paid internship associates, we can build a network of people who can expose us to the details of running a business and can mentor us as we start on our journey.

You can't be what you can't see. If you want to open a dry cleaner, then go find a dry cleaner where you can work. As I've mentioned, by working at paid internships, you can learn the systems they use and replicate the best of those systems when you open your own business. You also learn the thoughts, decisions, and habits from the owners who run those businesses. When I worked for Chuck Goldberg, or Ted Rafokolis at Lorenzo's, or when I supplied food to Charlie Robinson, I absorbed what they did and took those lessons with me. I also learned from their failures. When they said, "Ken, you shouldn't do this or that because it didn't work for me," I remembered their mistakes and tried not to repeat them.

Soaking Up Knowledge

The books they told me to read, I read. The people they told me to meet, I tried to meet. The habits they told me to develop, I tried to develop. I asked constant questions. With their answers, I possessed my knowledge plus their knowledge, and my confidence grew. Sometimes I would just hang around when they talked with other associates. I didn't always feel comfortable because I couldn't always contribute to the conversation; sometimes I had to sit there like a bump on a log. But as long as my mentors didn't mind, I stuck around. And just look at the result! My mentors allowed me to see what I could be. They grew my vision and my passion. Success is habitual, not accidental. We learn what has worked from others who have gone before us; we internalize those lessons until they're a part of us, and then we replicate them.

Formal Associations

Your loose network of associations is a key part to your success. But formal industry associations can also provide support and a fresh perspective. When I opened my restaurants, all my responsibilities sometimes overwhelmed me. I had vision, passion, and a wealth of preparation and experience in the food industry, but I needed on-the-job training in terms of financial management. In *The 7 Habits of Highly Effective People*, Stephen Covey says we need to constantly associate with people who are several steps ahead of us. When I started out, I knew almost nothing about spreadsheets, balance sheets, and P&Ls. To get the support I needed, and to learn from other successful McDonald's, I joined the National Black McDonald's Operators Association (NBMOA).

I learned just how vital professional associations can be to one's success. NBMOA is a self-help organization, established in 1972 to bring together African American McDonald's owners and suppliers to work for their advancement and the advancement of African American society as a whole.

As a new entrepreneur, I was a young man on fire with vision and passion. I came into the NBMOA meetings with a lot of questions, and I wasn't afraid to ask them. I was pumped to get new information. Although it was clear I had a lot to learn, before long I was asked to sit on the board of directors for the Michigan Region of NBMOA. Several people at our meetings seemed to feed off my energy, and I suppose they thought they could harness some of that by putting me on the board.

Within a few minutes of the first meeting as a board member, however, it was clear I had no idea what I was doing. Fellow board members talked way over my head. Worse, I hadn't used Robert's Rules of Order since my college fraternity days—it was a jumble of motions and bylaws and votes. During my paid internships, I learned to seek out opportunities to stretch and grow, and although I felt overwhelmed at NBMOA meetings, I knew I could learn a great deal from the experienced entrepreneurs in the room. I believe that if you're the smartest person in a group, then it's time to find a new group. So I sat in the NBMOA meeting and relaxed, listening to and soaking up knowledge from people who had far more experience and far more money than I possessed. I didn't need to be an expert to contribute. At first I couldn't add anything but passion, out-of-the-box thinking, and a willingness to ask questions. But that was still important. Sometimes I would ask something that seemed like a stupid question, but I would ask it anyway. After the meetings, sometimes people came up to me and said, "Man, I'm glad you asked that. I was wondering the same thing myself." My energy and willingness to be vulnerable gave voice to questions that other people also shared.

When I first joined NBMOA, Larry Tripplett was chairman and CEO of the organization. He was an ex-school principal and very organized. He would bring in people from other organizations and businesses to conduct workshops. Through his leadership and the workshops, I learned that I only owned the cash flow of the business, that I needed to have multiple streams of income, and that I needed to develop an exit strategy. Like my mother would do when she took us places to glimpse life beyond poverty, Larry Tripplett and NBMOA helped me look over the fence of my daily operations.

NBMOA also gave African American business owners a chance to stick together on certain issues McDonald's needed to address. For example, African American owners generally own stores in the inner cities, but there's a cost to operating in such places that suburban or rural McDonald's owners don't face. Security costs are higher—sometimes you have to hire private security or police to be visible during certain hours. Some owners have to lock their bathrooms, and then buzz customers in when they need to use them. Customers would steal the toilet paper, or worse, people would use the bathrooms to do drugs or engage in prostitution. The cost of insurance in an urban area was a lot higher. Inner-city McDonald's restaurants have typically outpaced the average McDonald's restaurant in sales, but those stores couldn't realize a proportional increase in their profits because of the added expenses. So NBMOA worked together to bring this problem to the corporate entities' attention.

Diversity

Financial planners typically advise investors to diversify their portfolio—to own stocks and bonds in a wide variety of companies and entities. The same can be said for our investments in our network of associates. We don't need to hang with, and do business with, the same type of people. That's one of the problems with corporations—large organizations seek similar people to hire, and then they train them to think and act alike.

Being an entrepreneur gives us the opportunity to meet people we wouldn't otherwise meet. Entrepreneurs are like-minded in terms of having vision and passion— in terms of being creative and taking chances—but they are incredibly diverse when it comes to knowledge and skill sets. Interacting with a diverse network of people gets you out of your comfort zone and offers you vast opportunities to learn and grow.

Plugging into a large and diverse network also makes you more valuable. You're a conduit to resources. If I coach someone who has questions about investing in real estate, I can connect him with a good friend of mine who is a prominent home builder. If someone in my mastermind group is interested in attracting capital for a new business idea, I can connect him with an associate who's involved in a community bank. By serving as a resource, you become valuable to others and gain a reputation as someone who is important to know. You build relationships and bridges to other business ventures. And you never know when a certain bridge may come in handy for your own future opportunities.

We can also develop strategic partnerships with people outside our business. As entrepreneurs develop more specialized businesses, and as Internet commerce continues to build, there are growing opportunities for entrepreneurs to team up. Entrepreneurs can conceivably outsource almost their entire operation. You might create a concept for a product, and then outsource its manufacturing, marketing, and distribution, not to mention outsourcing the administrative tasks (payroll, bill payment, bookkeeping, benefits, etc.).

If you've developed a network of trusted associates, you can hit the ground running with strategic alliances that will work toward a common vision. You can save yourself considerable investment in equipment, systems, and bricks and mortar by leveraging the investments and know-how of other enterprises.

In a way, that's how the Brown Food Group operated. I had the employees and the concept for how to operate a highly successful fast-food service, and the McDonald's Corporation had the buildings and equipment. We formed a strategic alliance—their assets and my entrepreneurial passion.

Giving Back

Forming a network provides great opportunities for receiving knowledge and advice. But it also provides opportunities for giving back—chances to bring together resources to help people.

One time I attended a workshop about credit education. A married couple ran the workshop. They were entrepreneurs who had formed a business—holding education and training sessions at corporations, schools, and churches. I was so impressed by the quality of their seminar (they made the information easy to understand and solutions simple to implement) that I hired them to put on a workshop for my staff.

I rented a hotel conference room and invited my entire staff to attend a session when they were off work. The only price of admission was a copy of their credit report. They had to bring the report and be willing to discuss it with the workshop leaders. The workshops were another part of my *people first* philosophy—my effort to remember my purpose by making a difference in the lives of my employees. The workshops were well attended, and I believe they did make a difference with my employees' finances.

The couple did seminars for other businesspeople in my mastermind group, and for several years, they had a good venture going—helping people recover from credit problems and earning a good income for themselves in the process. Then they received some terrible news—the wife was diagnosed with stage four colon cancer. They were entrepreneurs, and all of sudden, they couldn't focus on their business. The wife had to focus on fighting the disease, and her husband needed to focus on taking care of her.

I prayed one day for those good people, "Lord, what can I do to help them?" The answer that came back to me was: the mastermind group. I called several of the people within my network of colleagues and said, "This couple shouldn't have to worry about their business. They shouldn't have to worry about their rent, their gas bill, their light bill. As

> **Freedom Thought**
>
> *When you start to build your informal network, you want a diverse group of people. You don't just want people in your profession. You can start with family members and friends and then venture out from there.*
>
> *Is there a paid internship you could pursue where not only would you gain valuable knowledge but you would connect with valuable people?*
>
> *For your formal network, seek out industry associations that can help you get started and support you along your journey. Find relevant associations by talking with industry professionals.*

a community of brothers and business owners, we need to take care of this stuff."

And that's what we did. We divided up the expenses and covered what needed to be covered. That spoke to the power of an association of like-minded people. We were able to lift up a fellow entrepreneur without any one person taking on too much of a burden. As individuals, it's unlikely we would've been able to help that much. Developing good associations is a freedom principle, and in that case, we were able to give a fellow businessman the freedom to focus on the right thing.

NINETEEN
The Right Dream Needs the Right People

Paul faced a difficult decision—whether or not to leave his job and start a consulting business with two other colleagues. He had been meeting for lunch with two business friends once a week for a few years. The lunches started out as a mastermind group—a chance to talk over business and develop new ideas. Eventually, however, the conversations turned to leaving their jobs and starting a business together. Paul was excited about the possibilities, but he faced a significant deterrent to taking the plunge—his uncle.

Paul's uncle had retired after working for the government. He saw a job as something one had a duty to do—and personal fulfillment had nothing to do with it. Paul highly valued his uncle's opinion, and his uncle made no effort to hide his displeasure with his nephew's consideration of starting a business. "What about your family?" his uncle asked. "How will you provide for them? It's irresponsible."

Paul had done the right thing by connecting

with a group of like-minded businesspeople. Paul got pumped just talking with the other men. But his uncle was a discourager. He sapped the energy right back out of Paul.

Fortunately Paul decided to take a chance and start the business. It did quite well and after a few years, he considered it a success. After he had made the decision, he stopped talking to his uncle about it. His uncle still wanted to discuss it, but Paul couldn't handle the negativity. He had to put some distance between himself and his uncle. Paul understood that he couldn't focus on the business and absorb his uncle's pessimistic outlook at the same time. After a year, Paul's uncle accepted the decision and acknowledged that Paul had done the right thing. Today they are close again. But Paul probably would not have followed his entrepreneurial dream if he had not made a tough choice about his relationship with his uncle.

The Three *D*s You Don't Want

One of the most difficult decisions we have to make about associations is to minimize or eliminate the relationships that bring us down. We may be blessed with many friends, and many of them may be quite successful. But we have to take a close, objective look at the people we spend the most time with. Time has value. It is a type of currency. When we spend it, we give up a valuable resource, and in exchange for that resource, we receive something. Hopefully we receive encouragement and healthy advice, but that's not always the case.

If you're like most people, you spend a significant majority of time with a small group of family members and friends. It's the 80/20 rule: 80 percent of our time goes to only 20 percent of our close acquaintances. For those 20 percent, we must guard ourselves against the three *D*s of negativity—people who discourage, deplete, and destroy.

People who discourage are sometimes well-meaning (not always, but sometimes). They either don't want to see us get hurt (by taking a risk and failing), or they envy the possibility of our success. They will say little things that succeed in creating doubts in our mind, but they don't add anything that encourages. They simply say enough to take the energy out of our new ideas and dreams.

People who deplete take even more energy from us. After we spend time with them, we come away tired and maybe even hopeless. Depleters are often people who have a negative outlook. They are pessimists who live by the subconscious motto: *Misery loves company*. They expect things to not work out, and they would prefer you agree with them. People who deplete are worse than people who discourage because they leave us worse off than they found us. They give us a negative return on our invested time with them.

Finally, we have to guard ourselves the most against destroyers. People who destroy, obviously, are dangerous. Their thoughts and actions can permanently damage your reputation, assets, or physical well-being. Destroyers involve themselves in immoral or illegal activity, and they hope to drag you down with them. Your success is an affront to the decisions they have made. They would rather take you down than take an honest look in the mirror.

I know it's a hard thing to do, but to be an entrepreneur, you have to minimize your face time with the three *D*s. They can't be in your top five people, and they can't be among the 20 percent of friends and family where you spend 80 percent of your time. When I embarked on my journey to be an entrepreneur, I distanced myself from certain friends. It was a hard choice, but it was a choice I had to make. They were saying things like, "How are you going to do that? You don't have enough money. You don't have enough education. You're going to uproot your family and move them to Michigan to follow a fool's dream?" Becoming a business owner was going to stretch me, and I needed to have as much energy, optimism, and encouragement at my disposal in order to reach the next level. I couldn't hang with people who would detract from that energy, optimism, and encouragement.

It isn't always a negative influence that's the problem. Sometimes it's just the drama in the lives of people close to us. It's important to do everything you can to keep unnecessary drama out of your life. Anything that takes away from your passion and energy is a distraction. It could be a family member, a friend, or the personal life of an employee. If it's not drama that is vitally important to your life, then you must do your best to distance yourself from it. Some drama is unavoidable—if your spouse just lost her job and is struggling with short-term depression—then it's your job to love her and help her. But some people have an unhealthy attachment to drama. It seems to follow them wherever they go and whatever they do. You can't allow yourself to get sucked into their messes and distracted from your entrepreneurial vision. You have to get away.

Mary Got Away

We can turn to the Bible to see how getting away is important. When the angel Gabriel appeared and told Mary she would conceive God's child, Gabriel also told her that her cousin Elizabeth "has also conceived a son in her old age; and this is now the sixth month for her who was called barren. For with God nothing will be impossible."[1]

Mary knew her cousin was also experiencing something miraculous. They had a common bond. Elizabeth was also Mary's elder and was more experienced in how to handle life's challenges. So Mary made a decision about associations. "Mary arose in those days and went into the hill country with haste, to a city of Judah, and entered the house of Zacharias and greeted Elizabeth."[2] With *haste*, she left the people who would not understand what was

---
1. Luke 1:36–37.
2. Luke 1:39–40.

happening to her. There were very strict laws about relations with a man outside of marriage, and Mary ran the risk of being severely punished, possibly even stoned to death because of her pregnancy. She did not need to be around the people of her town with God's vision now growing inside of her. Instead, she went to the one person who would understand. Elizabeth was more experienced in the world and was six months along in her own pregnancy when Mary became pregnant. She was several steps ahead of Mary, and Mary needed to associate with her during that vulnerable time.

When she arrived at Elizabeth's home, Mary greeted her cousin. "And it happened, when Elizabeth heard the greeting of Mary, that the babe leaped in her womb; and Elizabeth was filled with the Holy Spirit. Then she spoke out with a loud voice and said, 'Blessed are you among women, and blessed is the fruit of your womb!'"[3] Something spiritual happened between the two of them. Not only did Elizabeth have no urge to condemn or stone Mary but Elizabeth rejoiced. She *understood* Mary and what was happening to her. She was an empathizer and encourager and not a discourager, depleter, or destroyer.

We have to make the same choices sometimes. When we're vulnerable, or when we're pregnant with a new vision, we have to be careful whom we associate with, including the closest members of our family. That doesn't mean we cut them out of our lives. Mary didn't

---
3. Luke 1:41–42.

run away forever. But she did stay away for a significant period of time—enough time for her to get her bearings and know what needed to be done. She stayed *away* from the people who could get in the way of God's plan, and she stayed *with* the person who could support God's plan.

Hanging with the wrong people is a very common reason for the avoidance of dreams. Entrepreneurial dreamers want to pursue the vision in their heart, but their associations get inside their head and say no. The other day I saw a T-shirt that said: "If you're still chasing your dream, you're running too slow." Those voices of doubt drag us down and make us move too slowly. But Mary ran with "haste" to Elizabeth's. She knew she needed to get away quickly—for her own safety, but also to make sense of things. As long as we open ourselves to the wrong influences, our dreams will remain forever out of our reach.

While discussing ownership, I mentioned the need to control your personal brand through your actions and appearance. But your associations also affect your brand. When people behave in morally deficient ways, it's usually with the support, and sometimes, company of their associations. When Michael Phelps damaged his personal brand by smoking pot at a college party, he did it with the support of the friends and partiers around him.

Ecclesiastes 7:1 says: "A good name is better than precious ointment." In the days of the Bible, ointment was an extremely luxurious product—it was very expensive and a treasured possession. But Solomon says our reputation—our personal brand—is even more valuable. When you want to borrow money, it is said that banks look to see if you have capacity, collateral, and character. When I opened my two restaurants, McDonald's loaned me $3 million. I didn't then have the capacity to repay the loan (one of the stores was brand-new and the other was underperforming), and I had absolutely no collateral. All I had was my character, my brand. But McDonald's considered that worth $3 million.

The McDonald's franchise agreement included a morality clause that required its franchisees to behave in a morally proper way. It's a similar clause to what professional athletes must agree to for their sports and endorsement contracts. How much was Phelps's character worth? In current and future endorsements—a whole lot more than $3 million. It was all jeopardized by the people he hung out with. Millions and millions gone because of his associations.

The Right Employees

As an entrepreneur, the associations you build with people a step or two behind you are just as important as those a few steps ahead. It's very important that you hire people who will latch onto your vision. You don't want yes men as managers, but you do want people who share enough common traits with you to see and follow the vision. A good relationship with an employee is like a good relationship with a spouse. Healthy marriages are made from two people who have separate and unique personalities but also share common values and vision for the future. Neither the husband nor the wife is afraid to raise objections to a decision with the other, but their differences rarely show up when deciding what values are most important.

When you hire the right people—when you value them and listen to them—you have the opportunity to build trust over time and build those familylike relationships. In order to honestly believe in your business, you must sell a product or service you believe in. But you must also employ people you believe in. They are an integral part of your overall product. They must share your work ethic and business philosophies because your customers will see those as much, or more, than they will see your own work ethic and business philosophies. At my core, I knew the people working directly for me would represent my business the way I wanted it represented.

Associations are all about strategic relationships. And what can be more strategic than the people who interact with our customers and sell our products? They are our face to the public. As a business owner, I wanted to have associates, not employees. I wanted to have partners in the vision. Employees will work to the minimum effort. Employees won't care about how they talk to your customers. But associates who understand your vision, and who are valued, will feel like they have some skin in the game.

It takes teamwork to make your dream work, but it takes an investment in time and energy to build a team. When I opened my new store, it took several months before my team worked efficiently. It was chaotic at first. That was the searching stage—the phase when I was searching for the right combination of people and the right roles to assign them. I was looking for competencies and how those skills fit into the jobs I needed to fill. There were plenty of growing pains. Mistakes were made. Transaction times took too long sometimes, and occasionally customers received the wrong order. People were working to gain confidence in their jobs, but they didn't understand the other jobs and couldn't work together as a team.

Gradually I found the synchronicity. That's when we entered the alliance stage—the phase when everyone knows their gift and their role, and they know how to interact as a team. Everyone is aligned, on the same page, and dedicated to your vision.

I believe everyone has unique gifts, and it's our job as entrepreneurs to uncover those gifts and honor them by putting them to work. That's not always an easy job. Society trains us to look at people from the outside. Movie stars and everyday people spend a fortune on looking good on the outside. It's what we use to make our initial impressions. But as entrepreneurs, we have to look at people from the inside.

That doesn't mean I have to hire someone wearing braids if I don't think that's appropriate. But sometimes the most impressive people come in the most unassuming and ordinary packages. Cynthia, whom I wrote about in chapter 9, didn't look the part of a store manager when I hired her. But she grew into the job, and I gradually saw her amazing strengths.

It's just like the "Acres of Diamonds" story I mentioned earlier. The main character in the story wanted to find the acres of diamonds and searched the world to find them. In the end, he died without ever making the discovery. Another man who bought the land from the diamond-searcher ultimately found a diamond buried under the dirt of his farm. It wasn't found in some glamorous locale, but at home. Even then, however, the diamond wasn't identified. It was thought to be just a shiny rock. Its brilliance was unknown until the priest recognized its true value. As leaders, it's our job to uncover the brilliant employees that sometimes lie beneath unglamorous surfaces.

> **Freedom Thought**
>
> *Who do you spend most of your time with? Who are your top five people? Although it can be very difficult, we must get away from people who will discourage, deplete, or destroy us. We must be like Mary, who fled from potentially damaging people and ran with haste to someone who would understand and support her.*
>
> *The same principle applies for our employees, contractors, suppliers, or other service providers. We must work with people who will support our dream and not distract from it with excessive drama or damaging behavior.*
>
> *We need the right people, so our visions can move forward, and eventually so our businesses can thrive after we're gone.*

The Last Associate

Whenever I went to a Major League Baseball game, I enjoyed

watching the athletic gifts of the nine players on the field. But those teams were much more than those nine players—they were also the players on the bench and the pitchers in the bullpen. Even more, they were the Minor League teams that trained the future stars and promoted them when they were ready. Major League clubs constantly work to develop future talent and to prepare players to replace the ones currently playing.

I noticed the same strategy when I worked for the McDonald's Corporation. They developed their bench strength and created a succession plan. After watching how it worked, I could identify who would be next in line for various top positions—for the CEO, COO, and different corporate vice-president positions. When a CEO retired, McDonald's was always prepared to move the next person into that position and move another person to replace the new CEO.

Business owners also need to develop an exit strategy and a succession plan. As I covered earlier, too many entrepreneurs get stuck because they lack those plans. They spend so much energy working *in* their business instead of *on* their business that they paint themselves into a corner. They can't leave and move on to the next level. The business depends on them too much. If they leave, the business will fail, and they feel trapped.

One of the most important associations you need to develop is your last association—your successor. To grow your business beyond yourself, you will need to develop systems and people who will function without

The Right Dream Needs the Right People

you. When you leave, who's going to do your job? How are you going to prepare them to do that?

During my last few years of owning the restaurants, I worked with specific people to develop them into my successors—to mentor them and transfer my knowledge. Although I would ultimately sell the stores to someone not yet involved in the business, I knew I could leave behind a self-functioning operation that would sustain my legacy and make my stores more attractive to purchase. The managers I worked with didn't have to be mirror images of me, but we had to share core values and buy into the same vision. To prepare them, I had them shadow me throughout the day. I conducted role-playing exercises with them. I had high-level conversations about strategy with them. I took them to meetings with associates outside of my operations.

When it was time for me to sell, they were prepared to carry my legacy forward. I was proud of the business we had built together, and I was proud to call them my associates.

Final Freedom Thoughts
Green and Growing

After my first year of McDonald's ownership, I attended a McDonald's awards banquet for the Michigan Region. As Ray Kroc would say, I was green and growing—but I was very heavy on the green side. I had begun my ownership experience with my guns blazing; I was filled with passion and a burning desire to do things differently. But I had no expectations of winning any awards. I still had too much to learn.

So I was shocked when the speaker announced the Rookie Owner of the Year award, and then called out "Ken Brown!" Later in the evening, I was shocked again when the speaker called out "Ken Brown!" for Most Outstanding Restaurant (awarded to my Ten Mile and Telegraph restaurant). I was stoked. My passion, creativity, and integrity had won over the awards committee.

However, the years ahead would bring many obstacles and difficult decisions. There would be many opportunities to lose my love for running a restaurant—to succumb to just getting by and not living in true entrepreneurial freedom. I made plenty of mistakes, as all entrepreneurs do, and I got myself into some tight situations. But I also held true to the freedom principles of entrepreneurial success. I kept my faith, stayed focused on my vision, remembered my purpose, fed my passion, took ownership of myself, and developed my associations.

In 2009, before I sold my restaurants, I attended one last awards banquet. That year, I received the Most Outstanding Restaurant award for my other restaurant—the one located in Southfield. And my manager, Robert Smith, won Most Outstanding Manager. I was equally proud of both of those awards.

I learned a lot during my journey through the arches—my journey through entrepreneurship. I hope you can examine my story and see a guy who came into business with no money, found a philosophy and system that worked, and exited while on top of his game. I hope you can take the lessons I learned and the actions I took and replicate them for success with your dreams.

You were born with what you need for success. You were born to be creative. You were born to be fruitful, to fill the earth, to be expansive, to conquer the obstacles that confront you. At the very beginning of creation, God gave you the divine spark you need to be an entrepreneur.

LIFE stands for Living In Freedom Everyday. There's no better way for you to experience life than to be an entrepreneur and to control your own destiny. Business plans, capitalization, and marketing strategies will play key parts in achieving your dreams. Some things you will know before you start your business. Other things you will have to learn as you travel along the journey. But as long as you adhere to the freedom principles—faith, vision, purpose, passion, ownership, and associations—you will succeed.

My LIFE through the arches gave me an amazing journey. I know your adventure through entrepreneurship will be just as rewarding.

Go out and live in freedom!

Go out and conquer your dreams!